A Fly-By-Wire Architectu[r]
Threaded Windows Apps

How to develop complex but reliable Windows applications quickly

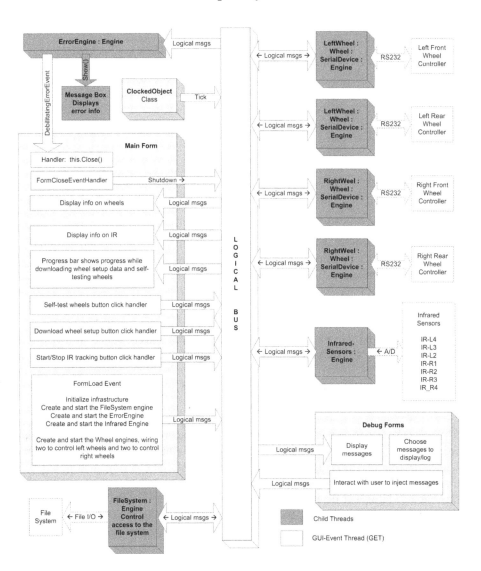

By Will Warner

The code for a complete demonstration Windows application—FBWwinAppDemo—written in C# accompanies this book. To download the source code, go to flybywirewinapps.com.

Portions of Chapter 4 are taken from material that previously appeared on Dr. Dobbs, www.drdobbs.com. Used with permission.

ISBN: 1475031742
ISBN 13: 9781475031744
Library of Congress Control Number: 2012904715
CreateSpace, North Charleston, SC

To my lovely wife, Nancy, for her
support and encouragement, and for the
marvelously apt term "unconditional
programming"

A Fly-By-Wire Architecture for Multi-Threaded Windows Apps

How to develop complex but reliable Windows applications quickly

Table of Contents

Introduction

This book presents techniques for structuring multi-threaded Microsoft Windows applications. It teaches how to use those techniques to develop complex but reliable Windows programs quickly. The only prerequisites are an understanding of object-oriented programming and some familiarity with Windows application development.

Well-behaved Windows programs that perform lengthy processing or that wait for stimulus or information from outside of the program make use of multiple threads. They must. For, otherwise, the program will be slow to repaint its Graphical User Interface (GUI), after dragging or being uncovered, will be slow to respond to input from users, and will generally degrade the performance of the computer that is executing it. The architecture I present makes the design of a multi-threaded program easy and straightforward.

The code for a complete demonstration Windows application—FBWwinAppDemo—written in C# accompanies this book. The same could be rendered in VB.Net or any sufficiently advanced object-oriented programming language. To make the demonstration interesting, we imagine that FBWwinAppDemo controls a simple robot that can sense the infrared radiation emitted by a person and follow him around a room. To download the source code, visit www.flybywirewinapps.com.

The dark box in the center of Figure I.1 represents the FBWwinAppDemo program in context. As appropriate for a context diagram, the box is empty, for it is just one of the components of the larger system. Figure I.2 depicts what will eventually fill that box. It is a diagram of the architecture of FBWwinAppDemo, the multitasking robot control program. My aim in this book is to bring readers slowly to an understanding of this architecture and prepare them to employ the concepts in their own Windows apps.

These concepts come out of my thirty-five years as a computer engineer working at the nexus of software and hardware. During these years, I saw develop in the minds of R&D managers the belief that modifying software is more fraught with difficulty than messing with circuitry. What they found is that because software is asked to do so much, it is very complicated. Because it is actually so easy to change and grow its functionality, software is often created without discipline. Vast, therefore, is the effort to verify its operation and prove that modifications to it produce no unintended changes in operation.

Many in product development are more comfortable with circuit diagrams (Figure I.3), which record designs in a form that is less opaque and easier to take in. Over time I began to incorporate concepts from digital circuitry in the design of software.

Digital circuitry comprises a number of nuggets of functionality—integrated circuit chips—suspended in a mesh of interconnections, and animated by, driven by, ticks of a clock. Internally, the ICs themselves are combinations of more primitive nuggets of functionality, which in turn are made from encapsulations of even more rudimentary capabilities.

At each level, encapsulations are "black boxes" to higher levels, their overall behavior specified, but their inner make up, internal connections, and operation invisible. The IC's external pins (Figure I.3) are its points of connection with the other components of the circuit; it is only the behavior at these connection points that is of concern to the designers of the circuit.

In addition, the ICs are interchangeable parts, so a design can employ as many copies of a part as are needed. Instances of the part behave identically. If different things come out of two of them, it is only because they received different inputs.

Early programming technique—the spaghetti code of the 1960s and even the structured programming of the 1970s—did not lend itself to picturing software in similar terms. But the emergence of object-oriented programming in the 1980s gave developers the concepts they needed to begin thinking in this way.

In object-oriented programming, a class is a nugget of functionality. Higher functioning classes derive from and extend the abilities of simpler ones or allocate and use simpler classes internally. The internal workings of the class, its private and protected methods and properties, are of interest only to the implementer of that class. Its public properties, methods, and events are analogous to the pins on the IC: they are the points of connection with the other components of the program.

Moreover, a programmer can deploy any number of instances of a given class. As with ICs, if different things come out of two instances, it is only because the two received different inputs.

Working at the junction of software and hardware also showed me the value of a fly-by-wire architecture. Fly-by-wire systems employ a local-area-network (LAN) as a backbone upon which to hang the major components of the system. The physical connection among them is only the wires of the LAN. The modules of functionality communicate by way of messages over the LAN.

I assume the term "fly-by-wire" comes from airplane design, which at some point replaced direct connection by cables between the ailerons on the wings and the pilot's stick, say, with a LAN that conveyed messages from embedded computers sensing movements of the stick to computers embedded with motors on the ailerons. Those messages describe what the aileron-controlling motors should do based on what the pilot does with the stick.

Automobiles today are fly-by-wire systems. The sensors (e.g., window up/down buttons) and actuators (e.g., window up/down motors) do not connect directly. They, along with all other devices in the car (including the radio) are modules on a LAN that snakes throughout the vehicle; they communicate using messages over the LAN.

Figure I.1: Context diagram for the FBWwinAppDemo robot control program. Using input from a bank of infrared radiation (IR) sensors, and under the control of FBWwinAppDemo, the robot will follow an IR source (a person) around the room.

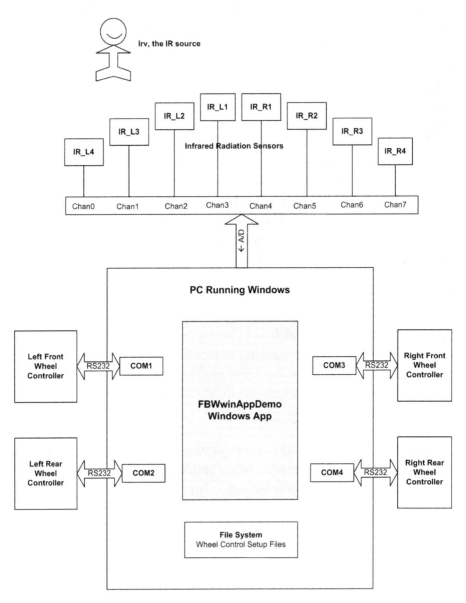

When a passenger presses the right-front-window-down button, that button sends a "right-front-window-down-button-pressed" message. The right-front-window up/down motor sees that message, and down goes the window. When the passenger lets up on the same button, the button sends a "right-front-window-down-button-no-longer-pressed" message. The right-front-window-up/down motor sees that message and stops lowering the window. Almost everything in the car works like this.

This way of operating gives a designer a lot of power to implement complicated features. For example, the car might contain a built-in telephone that sends a "phone's-ringing" message when the telephone begins ringing. The window-control motors on all windows could see that message and automatically roll up all the windows. The radio could see the message and turn down its volume. I'm not saying you would want the car to behave this way, only that it would be easy to do using the fly-by-wire methods.

My idea is to use the fly-by-wire concepts in complex Windows applications. I don't mean as part of a system in which the Windows app is one of the components, but rather within the Windows program itself. In such a program, the nuggets of functionality are classes that do most of their processing in child threads. These components of the program communicate using messages sent on the software equivalent of the LAN in fly-by-wire systems, that is, on a "logical bus" within the program itself. (Figure I.2.)

Using a logical bus over which the components of the program communicate makes possible a very powerful debugging and testing aid. The program may include a special component with its own GUI, whose job is to display and/or log messages that appear on the bus. This is analogous to "sniffers," devices that record and display communication between two devices over an RS232 connection, say. Being able to see who said what to whom, and when, is very helpful in debugging.

As developers, you can equip the debugging component's GUI with the ability to interact with you and interject messages, messages that will, eventually, come from a program element that is not yet implemented. This helps you test the program as you breathe life into it.

These techniques also assist with unit testing. If individual modules within the program function by responding to messages, unit-test code can stimulate the modules with those same messages and assess the response.

Another advantage to this approach is that the highest-level diagram of every fly-by-wire Windows app looks like Figure I.2. It is a collection of boxes representing nuggets of functionality, interconnected by the logical bus. Add as many boxes as you need, give them names that suggest their roles in the program, define the messages they send and the data the messages carry, and you've got your high-level design.

As seen in the diagram, this architecture makes use of another technique from digital circuitry, the clock. Ticks of the (software) clock drive processing and, especially, synchronize activity and communication among the various threads.

These programs rely very heavily on events to carry forward processing. This makes possible a style of coding I call "unconditional programming" because very little of the code will contain branches. Years ago we condemned the "goto" statement, and I now question the use of if-statements for the same reason: they add complexity to code, making it harder to understand and modify. I devote parts of this book to promoting a style of programming that minimizes the use of the if-statement.

Finally, I will make some potentially controversial observations about software development methodologies and incorporate my views on what constitutes elegance in software design.

The FBWwinAppDemo program presented here comprises two projects. One—WinAppInfrastructure—produces a dynamic-linked-library that furnishes the fly-by-wire infrastructure. The other project—RobotController—includes the forms and additional classes that make use of the infrastructure to achieve the functionality required of the robot controller. Thus segregated, the FBW infrastructure is available to underlie any Windows application.

Figure I.2: FBWwinAppDemo Architecture. The program must simultaneously communicate with four wheel controllers and eight infrared radiation (IR) sensors.

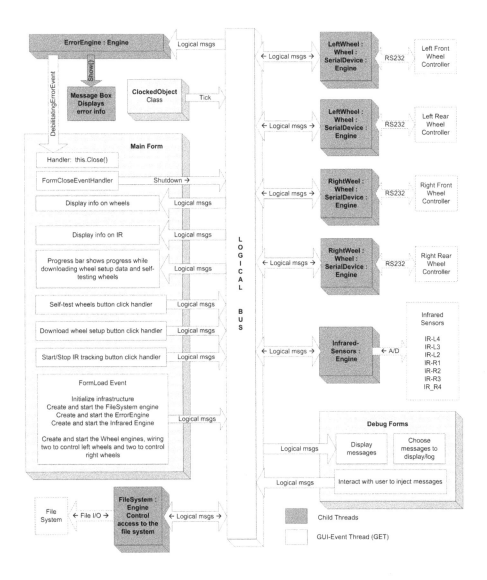

Figure I.3: An integrated circuit chip (IC) in a mesh of interconnections with other components of a larger circuit. The 10-MHz clock input drives its operation. The straight lines and easy-to-trace interconnections of circuit diagrams produce a feeling of understandability for many people.

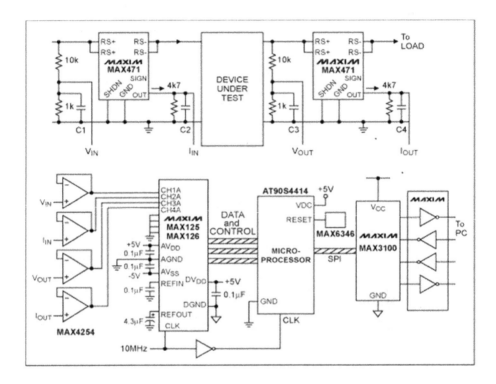

Notational Conventions

This book includes many diagrams of building blocks and assemblages. These diagrams employ shading and outline and direction of arrows to convey meaning.

3-D box representing a class or instance of a class

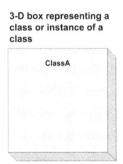

3-D boxes representing a class derived from a base class

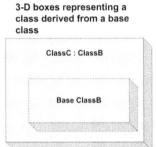

3-D boxes representing a class that allocates and uses another class

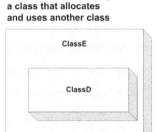

Components on drawings that are rendered in dotted lines are included to indicate context and are not part of what is being illustrated:

The direction of arrows indicates the source of initiation of an access by one component of another. Pointers within in the arrows indicate the direction of data flow:

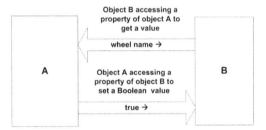

Arguments passed to methods are listed with parenthesis in arrows showing invocation of methods:

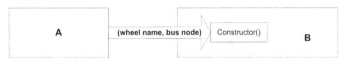

Use of shading to indicate execution context:

The names of program elements (classes and their properties, methods, and events) are rendered in a different font (e.g., `ObjectQueue`).

Chapter 1: Building Blocks

We begin with some basic concepts and simple building blocks that later chapters will elaborate and combine to form the complete fly-by-wire program, FBWwinAppDemo. I present each building block as a diagram and explain it. Each depicts a class found in FBWwinAppDemo.

1.1 Multi-Threading and the GUI Event Thread

If you are not already familiar with "threads," they are at first a little hard to understand. Think of a novel with two subplots or storylines. Typically the novel devotes alternating chapters to advancing each of the subplots. Chapter one introduces John and his problems. In chapter two we meet Marsha and begin her (seemingly) unrelated story. Chapter three takes us deeper into John's conflict. Chapter four moves Marsha's tale forward. And so on.

If the novel were an executing computer program, the story lines would be threads. A thread is a portion of the program that can run and do its work independently. People describe threads as performing "parallel processing" or doing two or more things "at the same time." Even if the processing is not literally occurring in parallel, it appears to be, and you can think of it that way.

A computer program runs under the control of the computer's operating system, or OS. The OS juggles the threads as they vie for execution time. It permits one thread to run for a short period of time, suspends it to give a slice of time to another thread, suspends that one in favor of another, ad infinitum.

Every thread periodically gets a little time in which to execute. During its time-slice, the code running in a given thread advances its storyline independently of the others. We speak of the execution that occurs in a given thread as taking place in the *context* of that thread and the reallocation of execution time as *context switches*. Because switches in context happen very rapidly, every thread gets to do its thing for a little while fairly often, so the processing they all do appears to be going on at the same time.

Why use threads? Why not write one monolithic program to do it all? You could, but it's likely to be one very complicated program. You will need a scheme—a single flow of execution—that gives as a much attention to each of the program's tasks as is necessary to make each come off as it should. Imagine John's and Marsha's unrelated subplots intermixed in every chapter, or within every paragraph, or every sentence. It is much better to write out their complete story lines, and then chunk them into comprehensible segments recounted in alternating chapters.

Well-behaved threads have themselves suspended—they sleep—whenever they find that what they need to continue processing is not immediately available. When a suspended thread resumes, execution picks up right where it left off, with the first statement following the statement that put the thread to sleep. Because other threads run while a given one is suspended, a thread can wait as long as it needs for something, without monopolizing the CPU. The rest of the program of which the thread is a part, and all the other running programs, will not be (seriously) affected.

When Windows launches your program, it creates a single thread in which to process all the events of your graphical-user-interface, your GUI. All the code you write to handle events from the controls on your GUI (e.g., button clicks, combo box selection changes, check box check changes) runs in this thread. I will call it the GUI-Event Thread, or the GET.

Because Windows uses a single thread to run all of your GUI event handlers, they cannot preempt one another. The button-click event handler must complete its processing and return, before the combo box selection-changed event handling code can run. So far, so good.

Your GUI forms also respond to events from Windows to repaint themselves. Unless you override it, code in the base class of a form handles this event. (What needs to be done to repaint is pretty esoteric; it is best not to mess with it and let the handler in the base class deal with it if you can, and usually you can.) Windows raises the `Repaint` event in a form whenever the form must resize, is dragged, or is uncovered.

Note that `OnPaint` is an event of your GUI, so it runs in your GET. This means it cannot preempt processing in your other event handlers. So if your button-click logic takes a long time to complete, your program will appear to be dead, hung, because it will not repaint, or respond to any other clicks or keystrokes, or even update the look of its cursor.

So what are you to do with the lengthy processing needed when that button is clicked? You have to get a child thread to do it. (The best example of processing that can take an unpredictably long time is database access, especially across a LAN; database access must be handled by a child thread.)

The button-click handling code must hand off any lengthy processing duties to a child thread and return. That's right: return. It can't wait for the processing to complete; it has to return. Otherwise it might have just gone ahead and done the processing itself. The `Repaint` event cannot occur until the button-click event handler returns.

If the form will display the results of the processing, or is otherwise affected by it, your code behind the form must include a handler for an event initiated by the child thread when the processing is done. That event must come in the GUI-Event Thread, not in the context of the child thread, because the form's controls can be touched only by code running in the GET. Making all of this easy and understandable is in large part what this book teaches.

The techniques I present also isolate and mitigate other potential problems inherent in multi-threading.

Threads must be careful not to step on each other's data. If a thread working on some data is preempted by another thread that also touches that data, there is potential for trouble. Threads that share data must protect themselves by locking access to that data while they work with it. Later chapters of this book present classes—`ProtectedObject` and `ObjectQueue`—that automatically afford this protection.

Isolating the use of locking in this way reduces the threat from another malady of multi-threading, namely, deadlocks. Threads block (suspend execution) when they attempt to secure a lock on an object that is already locked by another thread. When that other thread releases its lock, the first thread obtains its lock and proceeds with its processing.

Deadlocks occur when, due to unfortunate timing, thread A locks object X, thread B locks object Y then blocks waiting to lock object X, and thread A blocks waiting to lock object Y. Both threads are blocked waiting for the other to release a lock that neither can release because both are suspended.

The following sections develop techniques that aid in sharing data among threads, avoiding deadlocks, and deferring processing to child threads.

1.2 Object Queues and Protected Objects

An `ObjectQueue` (Figure 1.1) holds and relinquishes objects. It provides methods for adding objects to the queue (`Enqueue`), for retrieving queued objects (`Dequeue`), for discarding all the objects in the queue (`Purge`) and for retrieving all the objects in the queue (`DequeueAll`). Method `Dequeue` removes objects from the queue in the order they were added. Dequeue returns the object still in the queue that has been there the longest. DequeueAll furnishes a list of all the objects then in the queue in the order they were enqueued.

An instance of ObjectQueue enqueues and dequeues in a manner that is safe for use by more than one thread. That is, one thread can enqueue objects and another dequeue them. Logic inside the ObjectQueue does what is needed for the safe sharing of objects between the threads.

In a way, an instance of an ObjectQueue has a foot in each thread. It is the portal of data flow between them. But data flows only one way in a particular instance of an ObjectQueue. A thread is either the "enqueuer" of the "dequeuer." For data to go both ways, the threads need to share two instances of the ObjectQueue.

Figure 1.1 illustrates the sharing of objects between two threads using an ObjectQueue.

The ObjectQueue is similar to a device used in digital circuitry, the *optical isolator*. One side of an optical isolator is wired into a low-voltage circuit; the other side resides in a high-voltage circuit. The two sides exist in different realms, if you will. Through the optical isolator, the low-voltage circuit can affect the high-voltage circuit, but the medium of communication between them is light. This provides complete electrical separation between the low-voltage and high-voltage sides, the necessary isolation of the realms.

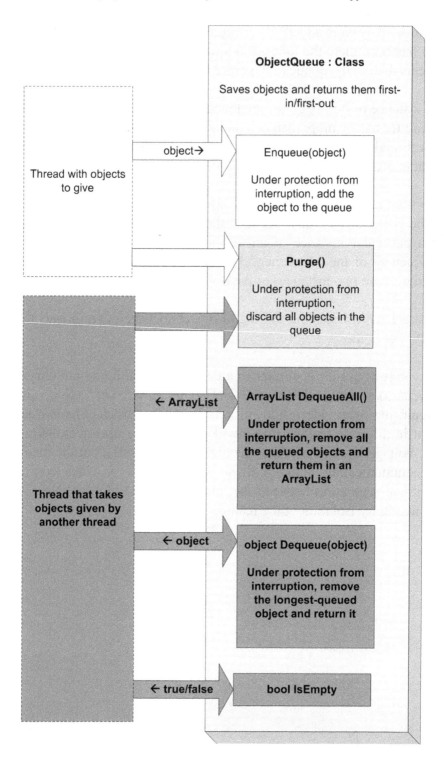

Figure 1.1: An `ObjectQueue` works as a portal of data flow between one thread and another. (Code: `WinAppInfrastructure.ObjectQueue.cs`)

Even though the `ObjectQueue` takes in and hands out objects in a multi-threading-safe way, logic in the enqueuing thread can still mess things up if it continues to manipulate the object after enqueuing it. Without taking care within the object to make possible safe access by two or more threads, the threads sharing the object can step on each other's work.

But rather than complicate these objects with logic to afford this protection, adopt the practice of enqueuing only objects that then go out of scope in the enqueuing thread. That is, enqueue only stack, or temporary, variables. Once they go out of scope in the enqueuing thread, they exist only in the queue, and later in the dequeuing thread, so there is no possibility of the enqueuing thread touching the objects while the dequeuing thread is working on them.

Figure 1.2 depicts the sharing of data between two threads using `ProtectedObject` and some of its derivatives. One thread writes an object into an instance of `ProtectedObject`, and another thread reads it out. The write and read take place under locking protection inside the `ProtectedObject` instance. As with objects passed to another thread through an `ObjectQueue`, the sending thread should leave the objects it writes alone after writing them, or problems may still occur.

Figures 1.1 and 1.2 illustrate that even though two methods are in the same class or module, they will not necessarily execute in the same thread. They execute in whichever thread invokes them. But because they are in the same module, they can access the same private variables. If these variables are instances of `ProtectedObject` or a derived class or of `ObjectQueue`, the access by multiple threads is safe because of the locking used internally by these classes.

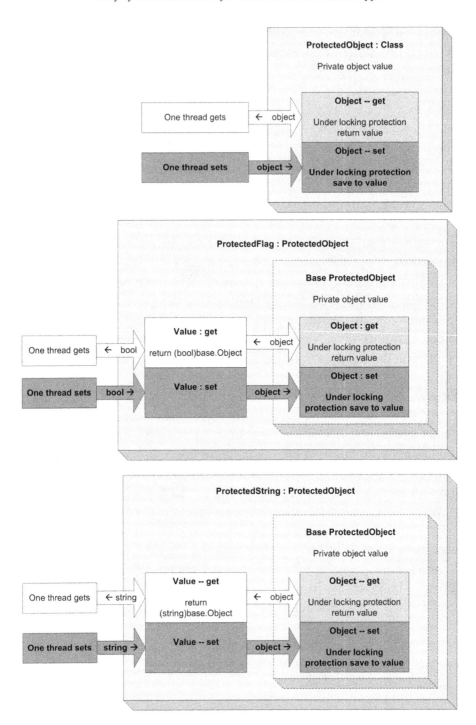

Figure 1.2: Instances of `ProtectedObject` help threads to safely hand each other objects. Classes derived from `ProtectedObject` permit the passing of specific types of data without having to cast the values. (Code: `WinAppInfrastructure.ProtectedObject.cs`)

1.3 Signals

Classes, of course, have properties and methods, but they also can expose *events*. An event is a feature of a class that provides notifications. Code that allocates an instance of such a class connects an *event handler* to its event. An event handler is just a method in some object in the program. It runs to handle the notifications—the events—when they occur. The events occur when logic within the event-bearing object *raises* them.

The fly-by-wire style of programming makes heavy use of events, so `WinAppInfrastructure` provides a class, `Signal`, which encapsulates and extends the event concept.

Code that is to run when a signal fires is linked as a handler for the signal:

```
// link handlers to run when the Start/Stop button is clicked
objIRCenteredSignal.LinkHandler(this.OnIRCenteredEvent);
objIRRightSignal.LinkHandler(this.OnIRRightEvent);
objIRLeftSignal.LinkHandler(this.OnIRLeftEvent);
objNoIRSignal.LinkHandler(this.OnNoIREvent);
```

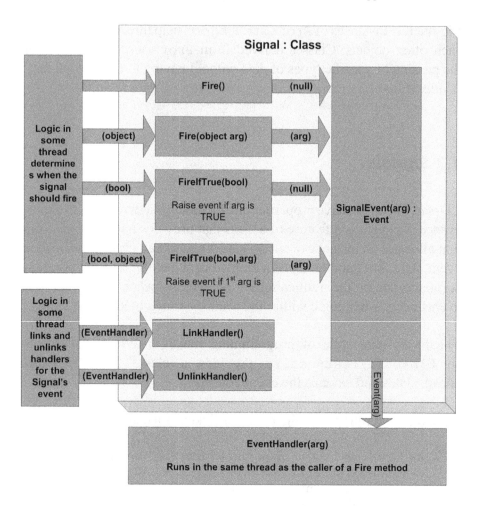

Figure 1.3: The `Signal` class encapsulates and extends events to provide notifications. Code that allocates an instance of `Signal` links a handler for its event. Other code invokes one of the `Fire` methods of the `Signal` object in order to have the event raised and, hence, the handler executed. (Code: `WinAppInfrastructure.Signal.cs`)

Two of the "fire" methods convey an argument from the code that invokes them on to the event handler. Two raise the event conditionally, that is, they cause the notification only when their Boolean argument is "true." Those two permit the code that invokes them to eliminate an if-statement. For example:

```
// notify when my queue is empty
this.mobjSignal.FireIfTrue(this.mobjQueue.IsEmpty);
```

replaces:

```
// notify when my queue is empty
if (this.mobjQueue.IsEmpty)
{
    this.mobjSignal.Fire();
}
```

The `Signal` class by itself does not help us communicate between threads. Its event handlers run in the same context as the code that invokes its `Fire` methods. The following sections present classes that build upon `Signal` to deliver events in the GUI-Event Thread, regardless of which thread invokes `Fire`, thus providing the means for child threads to excite processing in the GET.

1.4 The Clock and Clocked Objects

Similar to the way electronics employs a clock signal to drive state changes in digital logic, the FBW architecture uses ticks of a software clock to drive and synchronize processing and communication within the program, especially communication between the GET and child threads.

The way a child thread excites processing in the GET context is to arrange for an event to occur in the GET. The handler servicing that event runs in the GET context, not in the context of the child thread that initiated processing that led to the event.

Refer to Figure 1.4. On program launch, logic invokes the static `Initialize` method of the `ClockedObject`. That method allocates a `Timer`, sets its period, links its `Tick` event to its static `Clock` method and enables the timer. Classes derived from `ClockedObject` furnish a `HandleClockEvent` method. Logic in that method runs on the next clock tick after some other logic enables the instance of the clocked object. When that handler runs, it runs in the GUI-Event Thread. Classes `ClockedSignal` and `ClockObjectQueue` derive from `ClockedObject`.

Two advantages come from this. First, because the code behind a form that is servicing the event in sync with the timer tick runs in the GET, it may touch the controls on the form (`ListBoxes`, `ComboBoxes`, `DataGrids`, etc.), whereas code running in the child thread cannot. Second, code can be simplified when you know that all the logic behind a form will run as an event handler in the GET, meaning that none of the code in that module will be preempted by any other code in that module.

This code fragment creates the clock that drives processing within FBWwinAppDemo, initializing it to tick every 20 milliseconds. This method should be invoked in the GUI-Event context as the program loads.

```
public static void Initialize()
{
    // start the clock that drives the infrastructure
    tmrSync = new System.Windows.Forms.Timer();
    tmrSync.Tick += ClockedObject.Clock;
    tmrSync.Interval = ChildThread.MIN_DELAY;
    tmrSync.Enabled = true;
}
```

1.5 Clocked Signal

The `ClockedSignal` (Figure 1.5) class derives from `ClockedObject`. It will generate its `SignalEvent` in the GET once, after other logic arms it to do so. `ClockedSignal` furnishes two methods used by other logic to link and unlink a handler for the event raised by an instance of this class.

The class offers four methods that other logic invokes in order to arm it. Two take an argument that will go to the handler of the event when it occurs.

Figure 1.4: The `ClockedObject` base class underlies functionality that is advanced by ticks of the software clock. (Code: `WinAppInfrastructure.ClockedObject.cs`)

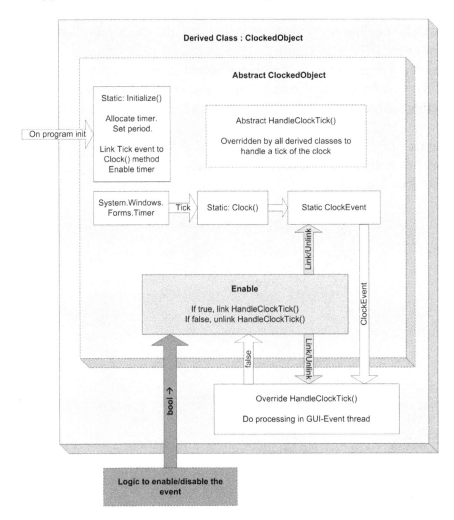

Two take a Boolean argument. If the argument is TRUE, the `ClockedSignal` object is armed to raise its event on the next clock tick. (Of course, the logic that invokes these `Signal` overloads could just refrain from invoking them when the argument it is passing is FALSE, but furnishing these overloads permits that other logic to be simpler.)

A `ClockedSignal` object overrides the `HandleClockTick` event of its base class, so its `HandleClockTick` method runs on every tick. When it runs, if the object has been armed by an invocation of any of its `Signal` methods, and a handler has been linked to the `SignaledEvent`, the tick-handling method raises that event, and the handler linked to it runs in the GET. The `SignaledEvent` passes an argument to the event handler. The argument is the object passed to the `Signal(argument)` or `Signal(bool,argument)` methods, or NULL if neither of these methods were used to arm the `ClockedSignal` instance.

Figure 1.5: `ClockedSignal` derives from `ClockedObject` and supplies notifications in the GET. (Code: `WinAppInfrastructure.ClockedSignal.cs`)

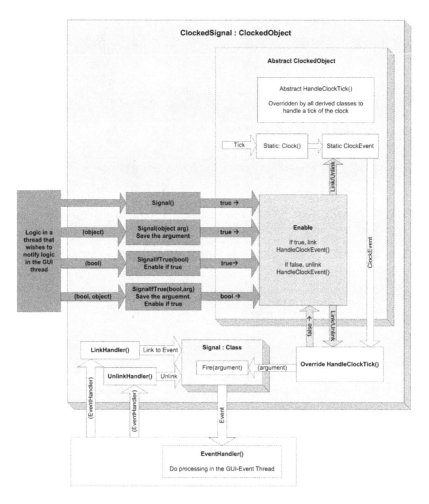

1.6 Clocked Object Queue

As shown in Figure 1.6, `ClockedObjectQueue` combines the features of the `Signal`, `ObjectQueue` and `ClockedObject` classes to queue objects and signal their availability to logic in the GET. Child threads queue the objects for processing, and event handlers run in the GET to process them.

Figure 1.6: Instances of `ClockedObjectQueue` generate events that announce the presence of objects in the queue.
(`Code: WinAppInfrastructure.ClockedObjectQueue.cs`

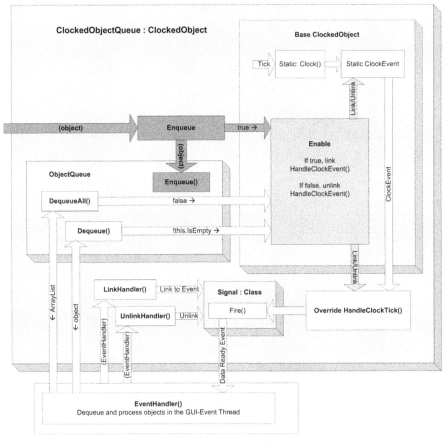

Class `ClockedObjectQueue` derives from `ClockedObject` and allocates instances of `ObjectQueue` and `Signal`. It overrides

HandleClockEvent. When that method runs (on a clock tick) it arms its SignaledEvent if the ObjectQueue is not empty, and then invokes its base.HandleClockEvent. That results in a SignalEvent, whose handler runs in the GET. This is one way in which a child thread passes an object to the GET for processing.

For example:

```
// allocate a message queue
static ClockedObjectQueue sobjMessages = new
ClockedObjectQueue();

// link a handler to run on every clock tick while messages
// are in the queue
sobjMessages.LinkHandler(OnMessagesQueued);

// runs on every clock tick when there are messages queued
// for dispatching
private static void OnMessagesQueued(object objArg)
{
    // get all the messages ready for dispatching
    ArrayList arlMessages = sobjMessages.DequeueAll();

    // for each such message
    foreach (LogicalMessage objMsg in arlMessages)
    {
        // have all handlers of this message execute ...
    }
}
```

1.7 Blocking Object and Interruptible Delay

Use an instance of BlockingObject (Figure 1.7) to suspend a thread for a given amount of time or until another thread resumes it. Allocate it so that it is within the scope of two threads, A and B. When Thread-A needs notification from Thread-B to continue, it calls the AwaitNotification method of the BlockingObject instance. Thread-B gives the notification when it calls method Notify.

Thread-A invokes `AwaitNotification` with a timeout value if it will wait only so long for notification. The thread awaiting notification obviously cannot be the GET because that thread must not block.

Figure 1.8 illustrates the use of `Delay`, a derivation of `BlockingObject`. Any thread (other than GET) may employ an instance of this class to suspend itself for a given amount of time. The thread will resume after the specified time elapses or after another thread aborts the delay. In the former case, `Delay.Wait` returns TRUE; in the latter case, or if the program begins closing down while the delay is underway, `Delay.Wait` returns FALSE.

How does this differ from just calling the Windows `Thread.Sleep(timeout)`?
The advantage of using the `Delay` object is that it will abandon a long sleep when told to by another thread or when the program begins to close down so that a thread that should die can do so immediately, without having to wait out the entire delay time.

Figure 1.7: `BlockingObject` gives child threads the means to easily block awaiting objects from another thread. (Code: `WinAppInfrastructure. BlockingObject.cs`)

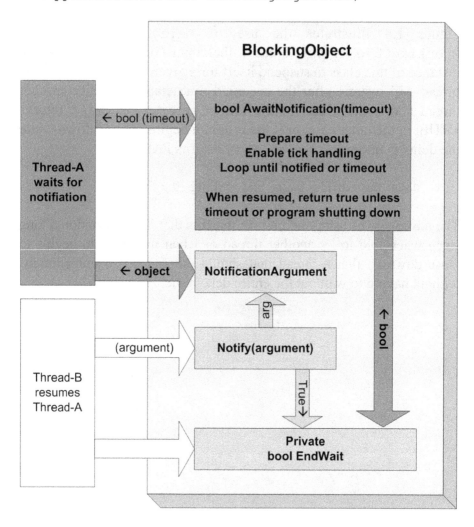

Figure 1.8: `Delay`, a derivation of `BlockingObject`, gives child threads the means to easily delay for a given period of time, but in a way that can be terminated early if the thread should die or because the program is shutting down.
(`Code: WinAppInfrastructure.Delay.cs`)

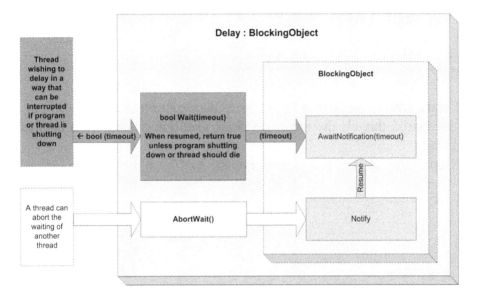

1.8 Blocking Object Queue

The `BlockingObjectQueue` (Figure 1.9) derives from the `BlockingObject` and incorporates an `ObjectQueue`. It provides an easy way for one thread to block waiting to dequeue objects enqueued by another thread.

A thread wishing to receive objects from another invokes `Dequeue` or `DequeueAll`. Either of those methods blocks if there are no objects currently in the queue. They return after another thread enqueues one or more objects or if the given timeout period elapses:

```
// a queue is allocated and visible to two threads
BlockingObjectQueue objJobs = new BlockingObjectQueue();

// one threads waits for things to be put in (5 secs, say)
ArrayList arlJobs = objJobs.DequeueAll(5000);
foreach (Job objJob in arlJobs)
{
     // ...
}
// another thread puts things into the queue
objJobs.Enqueue(objJob);
```

Figure 1.9: `BlockingObjectQueue`, derived from `BlockingObject`, gives child threads the means to block awaiting objects from another thread.
(Code: `WinAppInfrastructure.BlockingObjectQueue.cs`)

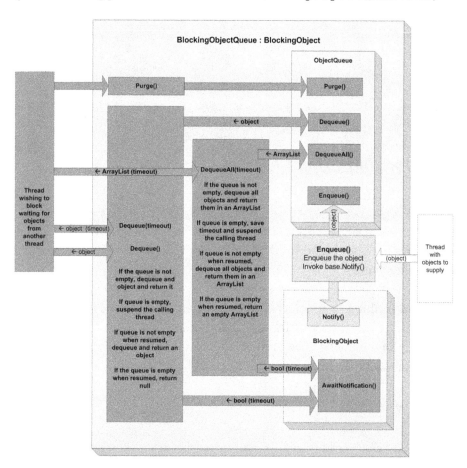

Chapter 2: Flying By Wire

This chapter combines and applies the building blocks of the previous chapter into the backbone of the fly-by-wire architecture.

2.1 Logical Bus and Bus Nodes

The singleton class `LogicalBus` (Figure 2.2) queues and dispatches messages. Messages derive from the base class `LogicalMessage`. "Dispatching" a message means raising an event to which are linked to one or more handlers for processing the message. Dispatching takes place on a Clock Tick event, so processing of the event occurs in the GUI-Event Thread.

The logical bus class maintains a list of registered message types. Its initialization method creates the list and adds to it the messages defined in WinAppInfrastructure. Typically the application will also define messages, which it will register by calling `LogicalBus.RegisterMessage`. The content of this list does not change after program initialization.

The logical bus class also maintains a list of registered message handlers. The list of message handlers is dynamic. Entries are added and deleted as the program wires and rewires itself during operation. Code registers a message handler for messages of a certain type from a certain source or to a certain recipient (Section 2.2). That code can later remove a message handler, and possibly register a different handler, appropriate for a new state of the program.

During initialization, the `LogicalBus` allocates a `ClockedObjectQueue` for holding messages to dispatch. It links a handler, `DispatchMessages`, to the queue's event that fires on every clock tick while the queue is not empty. This insures that `DispatchMessages` runs on every clock tick that occurs when the queue contains messages for sending. `DispatchMessages` dequeues all messages and, for each message, raises an event to which are linked all handlers currently registered for messages of that type—from a certain source or to a certain recipient. All of those handlers then run in the GUI-Event Thread, receiving the message object as an argument.

Logic anywhere in the program—in the GUI-Event Thread or any other thread—invokes `LogicalBus.Send(logicalMessage)` to send a message. The method enqueues the given message for dispatch on the next clock tick.

`LogicalBus` defines an enumerated type—`BusNode`—to identify code that is either the sender or named-recipient of a message. It defines explicitly bus nodes for engines (Section 2.6) created by WinAppInfrastructure (e.g., `BN_FILE_SYSTEM`, `BN_ERROR_ENGINE`). In addition, it defines twenty additional bus nodes for allocation to the application (`BN_APPL_1`, `BN_APPL_2`, etc.). During initialization, the application repeatedly invokes `LogicalBus.GetNextBusNode(node description)` to get bus nodes to use for uniquely identifying components of the application that send or receive messages. `LogicalBus` saves the bus node descriptions and uses them to identify the source or target node in descriptions of logical messages in debugging messages. The code in Figure 2.1 illustrates the technique.

You can think of the sender as a server of information and the recipient as a client. The server puts the information out there, not knowing which module in the code will act on it. Similarly, the recipient may not know which module of code has sent the message. Thus the sender and receiver do not need to be within each other's scope.

When a module of code must be identifiable as the sender or intended recipient of a message, it is assigned a bus node. Typically, an object's bus node is given to it as an argument to its constructor.

Figure 2.1: Code to illustrate how to obtain bus nodes for elements of an application

```
/// <summary>
/// Makes available bus node IDs for various program components
/// </summary>
internal class AppBusNodes
{
    // hold BusNode Ids for engines in the application and for
    // the progress bar
    static private BusNode senmProgressBarBusNode;
    static private BusNode senmIRSensorsBusNode;
    static private BusNode senmLeftFrontWheelBusNode;
    static private BusNode senmLeftRearWheelBusNode;
    static private BusNode senmRightFrontWheelBusNode;
    static private BusNode senmRightRearWheelBusNode;
}


//*******************************************************
///<summary>Invoke  once  on  program  load,  from  the  GUI
thread</summary>
//*******************************************************
internal static void Initialize()
{
    // get BusNode Ids for engines in the application and for the
    // progress bar
    senmProgressBarBusNode = LogicalBus.GetNextBusNode("Prog Bar");
    senmIRSensorsBusNode = LogicalBus.GetNextBusNode("IR Sensors");
    senmLeftFrontWheelBusNode = LogicalBus.GetNextBusNode("LF Wheel");
    senmLeftRearWheelBusNode = LogicalBus.GetNextBusNode("LR Wheel");
    senmRightFrontWheelBusNode = LogicalBus.GetNextBusNode("RF Wheel");
    senmRightRearWheelBusNode = LogicalBus.GetNextBusNode("RR Wheel");
}


//*******************************************************
// Accessors for the BusNode Ids assigned to parts of the application
//*******************************************************
static public BusNode ProgressBarBusNode
{ get { return senmProgressBarBusNode; } }
static public BusNode IRSensorsBusNode
{ get { return senmIRSensorsBusNode; } }
```

```
static public BusNode LeftFrontWheelBusNode
{ get { return senmLeftFrontWheelBusNode; } }
static public BusNode LeftRearWheelBusNode
{ get { return senmLeftRearWheelBusNode; } }
static public BusNode RightFrontWheelBusNode
{ get { return senmRightFrontWheelBusNode; } }
static public BusNode RightRearWheelBusNode
{ get { return senmRightRearWheelBusNode; } }
```

2.2 Logical Messages

Logical messages are classes derived from the `LogicalMessage` base class (Figure 2.3). A message is a mechanism for conveying data, or just notification, from one part of the program to another. The sender and recipient do not need to know of each other.

The constructor of a message object may take a bus node as an argument. Depending on the message, the bus node may identify the sender or the intended recipient. There is no provision for specifying both in a single message type.

Logic that wishes to receive messages of a given type registers a handler for them (Section 2.1). The registration may name a bus node that is either the sender or the intended recipient of the message in addition to the method that is to handle the message. Or the registration may be for any instance of the given message type, regardless of the sender. Message handlers run on the clock tick following the sending of a message.

The constructor for most message objects accepts an object known as a *payload*. The payload is made available to handlers that process the message. It can be anything; the only requirement is that the sender and receiver agree on what kind of object the payload is.

For example, the following line of code allocates and sends a message bearing a job as its payload to the module that controls access to the file system:

```
new EnqueueJobMsg(BusNode.BN_FILE_SYSTEM, objJob).Send();
```

The following code registers a handler—HandleFileSystemJob—for the message:

```
// route file system job msg to a method to process them
LogicalBus.RegisterMessageHandler(typeof(EnqueueJobMsg),
this.HandleFileSystemJob, BusNode.BN_FILE_SYSTEM);
```

Before code can go completely out of scope and be disposed, it must remove its message handler registrations. The following code removes the registration accomplished by the code just above:

```
// remove the handler for job msgs sent to the file
// system
LogicalBus.RemoveMessageHandler(typeof(EnqueueJobMsg),
this.HandleFileSystemJob, BusNode.BN_FILE_SYSTEM);
```

Figure 2.2: The `LogicalBus` queues and dispatches messages.
(Code: `WinAppInfrastructure.LogicalBus.cs`)

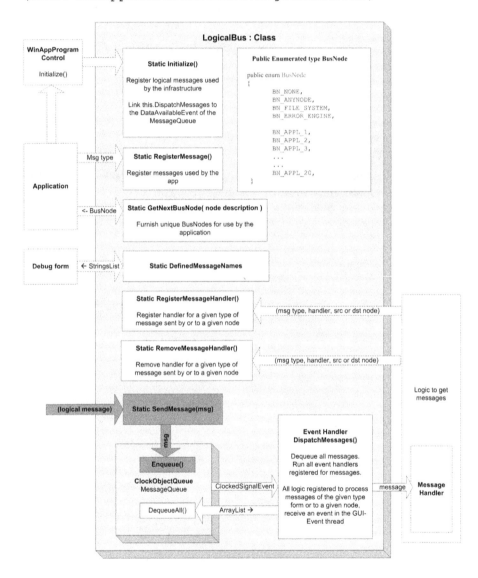

Figure 2.3: A hypothetical logical message derived from the abstract `LogicalMessage` base class. (Code: `WinAppInfrastructure.LogicalMessage.cs`)

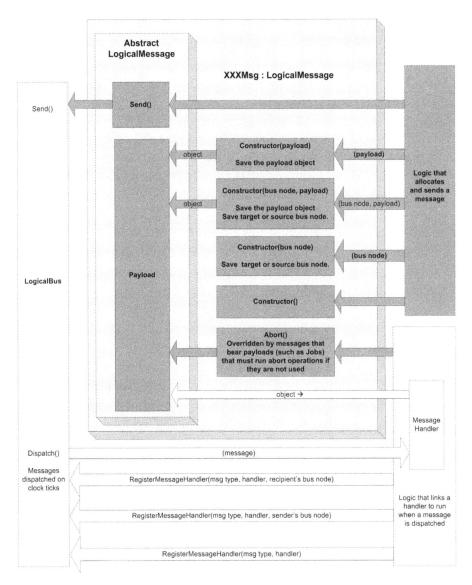

2.3 Child Threads

Look again at Figure I.2. The dark boxes represent *engines*. Engines (Section 2.6) do their work in the context of a child thread. A child thread is any thread created and set in motion by code running in the GUI-Event Thread.

WinAppInfrastructure furnishes a base class for child threads, `ChildThread` (Figure 2.4). Specific child threads derive from `ChildThread`. What makes them unique is the logic they include that is to run in the child thread context. Derived threads override method `GetThreadProc` to return what is needed to set up that logic as the code that runs in the child thread context.

Code running in the GET allocates a class derived from `ChildThread` then invokes its `Start` method. The child thread begins to execute its logic. To stop the thread in an orderly way, logic anywhere in the program invokes the child thread's `Die` method.

The logic running in the child thread context can do anything it likes but should periodically check the `ShouldDie` flag in the `ChildThread` base class. That flag will test as TRUE if the thread has been told to die or if the program is shutting down. The base class also provides a method– `Delay`–that suspends the thread until a given number of milliseconds have elapsed. `Delay` returns early (returning FALSE) if the thread should die.

To illustrate, the following code would be well behaved as the logic of a child thread:

```
// method that runs in the child thread
private void ThreadProc()
{
    // keep processing until thread killed or program shut down
    while (base.Delay(1000))
    {
        new DebugMsg("Not shutdown yet").Send();
    }
}
```

2.4 Message Queues

A `MsgQueue` is a `BlockingObjectQueue` that holds messages of a given type sent to a given recipient. The constructor of a `MsgQueue` instance takes as arguments a message type and a target bus node. The constructor wires the instance to capture messages of the given type sent to the given bus node. Figure 2.5 depicts the construction and operation of a `MsgQueue`.

Logic running in child threads may use an instance of `MsgQueue` to capture messages sent to it. The logic can either poll the message queue (`DequeueMsg`) for a message, wait a given number of milliseconds for a message (`DequeueMsg(timeout)`), or wait indefinitely for the next message (`AwaitMsg`).

As logic running in a child thread exits, it may choose to purge the message queue. This will result in an invocation of the `Abort` method of each of the purged messages, which is done in case the senders of those messages need to know that the messages did not actually get processed.

These lines of code allocate a `MsgQueue` to trap `EnqueueJobMsg` messages to the first app bus node and wait for such a message to arrive:

```
// set up to trap EnqueueJobMsg messages to the first
// app bus node
this.mobjMsgQueue =
new MsgQueue(typeof(EnqueueJobMsg), BusNode.BN_APPL_1);

// wait the next message
LogicalMessage objMsg = this.mobjMsgQueue.AwaitMsg();
```

Figure 2.4: A hypothetical child thread derived from the `ChildThread` base class.
(Code: `WinAppInfrastructure.ChildThread.cs`)

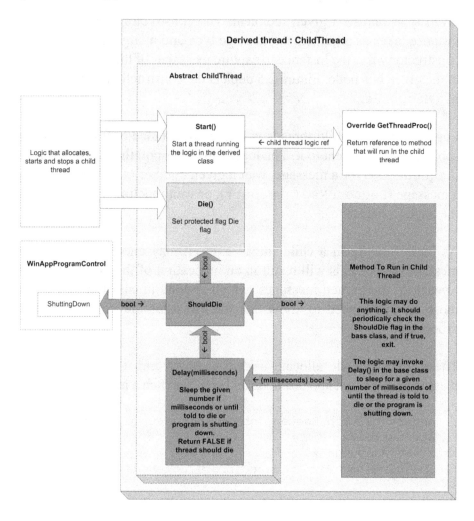

Figure 2.5: A `MsgQueue` traps messages of a given type sent to a given target node and queues them for processing. (Code: `WinAppInfrastructure.MsgQueue.cs`)

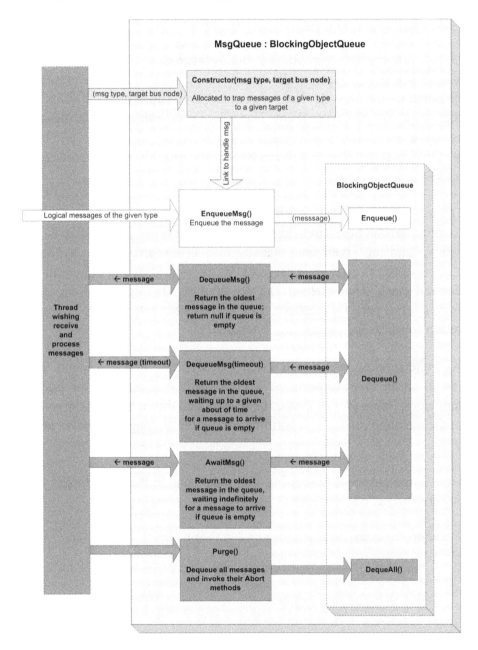

2.5 Message Processing Threads

MsgProcessingThread (Figure 2.6) extends the functionality of ChildThread. It is a child thread that processes logical messages.

Using arguments passed to its constructor, an instance of MsgProcessingThread allocates a MsgQueue to capture messages directed to the thread. The ProcessMessages method waits for messages and processes them. The actual processing of each message is done by ProcessMessage, which each class derived from MsgProcessingThread overrides with its special logic for processing a message.

Derived classes also override a property (MessageWaitTime) to provide the time (ms) to wait for the next message. If it is not infinite and the given time elapses without the arrival of a message, ProcessMessages invokes TakeProcessingOpportunity in the derived class. That method can do anything. It might poll for input from a serial port, for example. TakeProcessingOpportunity must return for message processing to resume.

As logic running in a thread exits, it purges the message queue. This results in an invocation of the Abort method of each of the purged messages. Some message types bear a payload through which the sender of the message can receive notification that the message was never acted upon.

Here is the message processing logic that runs in the child thread of a MsgProcessingThread:

```
// keep taking messages until the program is closing
while (!base.ShouldDie)
{
    // wait the next message
    LogicalMessage objMsg =
    this.mobjMsgQueue.DequeueMsg(this.MessageWaitTime);
```

```
// if got a message ...
if (objMsg != null)
{
   //...process a msg (code furnished by derived class)
   this.ProcessMessage(objMsg);
}
else if (!base.ShouldDie)
{
   // ...no message; do other processing
   // (code furnished by derived class)
   this.TakeProcessingOpportunity();
}
}
```

2.6 Engines and Jobs

An *engine* is a MsgProcessingThread that is fed messages whose payloads are *jobs*. Figures 2.7and 2.8 illustrate engines and jobs. Job classes encapsulate logic that is time consuming or blocks, so must run in a child thread.

An engine overrides the ProcessMessage method of its base MsgProcessingThread. The message processing loop in the base invokes an engine's ProcessMessage method, passing a logical message sent to the given engine by other code. That method extracts the job object from the message and invokes the Execute method of the job. That method does what is common to all jobs and then invokes an abstract method, ExecuteJob, which supplies the logic specific to the given job. After ExecuteJob returns, Execute does the rest of what is common to all jobs.

Job classes derive from the Job base class, overriding the base's ExecuteJob. Specific job classes have constructors that accept as parameters whatever information is needed for the processing they must do. You may also give them properties through which code can learn of the outcome and access any data produced by the processing.

Figure 2.6: `MsgProcessingThread` and derivations.
(Code: `WinAppInfrastructure.MsgProcessingThread.cs`)

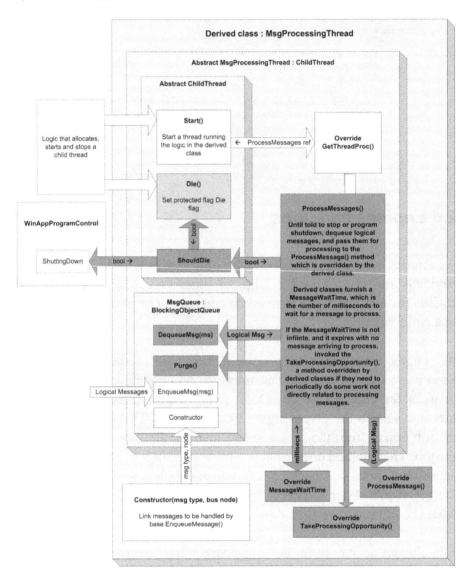

Generally, engine threads sleep while no jobs are pending for them. They can, however, specify a finite time to wait for the arrival of job-bearing messages and override the `TakeProcessingOpportunity` method of their base class. Should the wait time elapse with no jobs to process, the engine's `TakeProcessingOpportunity` will execute.

That method may do whatever you like. It may, for example, poll of input from an external device. Whatever it does, job processing by this engine will not resume until `TakeProcessingOpportunity` returns.

Engines execute jobs sequentially. There is no possibility of interrupting the current job merely by enqueuing the next job. This affords a natural sequencing mechanism that you may exploit to simplify your code. Often an engine abstracts a resource in the computer, a resource that may be shared by many of the components of your program. Perhaps it is a database, or merely a file, or an external device. It is useful to be able to depend on the fact that a dialogue with a resource, once begun, will complete before the next interaction with it begins.

The constructor of the `Engine` base class takes a bus node value as an argument. The bus node tells the engine its identity on the logical bus, that is, its identity within the FBW architecture. It uses this bus node to specify the source of messages it sends, if any.

The engine constructor also links handlers for messages directed to the engine. In particular it links handlers for the following logical messages:

* `EnqueueJobMsg`
* `CancelCurrentJobMsg`
* `GetEngineStatusMsg`

The base `Engine` class includes the handlers for all of these messages.

Use of jobs by code in the GUI-Event Thread

Code in any child thread or in the GET may allocate and queue jobs for processing by engines. When initiated by the GET, the code cannot wait for the job to complete, but it can link up event handlers to the job that will run in the GET when the job processing completes.

When a job completes successfully, fails, is canceled or aborted, it announces the end of processing by raising a number of events. These events occur in the GET. GET code that allocates and enqueues the job for execution links handlers for one or more of these events if notification is needed in any of these cases.

Figure 2.7: Engine and derivations (Code: WinAppInfrastructure. Engine.cs)

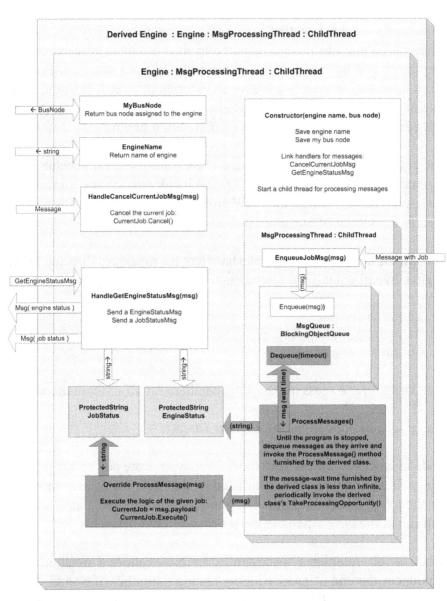

One event, `JobDone`, occurs as processing comes to an end, regardless of whether it was successful, failed, timed out, or was canceled or aborted. Sometimes that is all you need to know—that the processing ended. But there are also events for each of the ways processing can cease: `JobSucceeded, JobFailed, JobCanceled, JobAborted`. One more event, `JobNotSucceeded` signifies any end to processing that is not success. Sometimes all you need to know is that the job succeeded or did not succeed, and can respond to all the forms of nonsuccess in the same way.

These features of the job class enable you to link specific logic to respond to specific outcomes of the work done by the job. If you need to do one thing when a job completes successfully, something else when it fails, and another thing if it is canceled, you can link different handlers to run in each of these cases. True, you could link one handler to the `JobDone` event, and in that handler test the properties of the job just ending its work to learn what happened, but this will unnecessarily riddle your code with if-statements. Better to have the job let you know what happened and have code ready in handlers to process each case.

For illustration, the following code fragment queues a job to be executed by the engine that does X and gets notification when the job ends its work. The code does one thing if the job succeeded in doing X, and does another thing for all the other cases (aborted, canceled, failed):

```
//********************************************************
///<summary>Handle a click on the DoX button</summary>
//********************************************************
private void btnDoX(object sender, EventArgs e))
{
    // indicate "busy"
    this.Cursor = Cursors.WaitCursor;

    // allocate a job to do X
    JobToDoX objJob = new JobToDoX ();
    objJob.JobSucceeded.LinkHandler(this.HandleXSuccess);
    objJob.JobNotSucceeded.LinkHandler(this.HandleXNotSuccess);

    // enqueue the job for execution
    new EnqueueJobMsg(enmBusNodeOfXDoer, this).Send();
 }


//********************************************************
///<summary>Runs when X succeeds</summary>
///<param name="objArg">The job that did X</param>
//********************************************************
private void HandleXSuccess(object objArg)
{
    // indicate "not busy"
    this.Cursor = Cursors.Arrow;

    // handle success of X
    …
}


//********************************************************
///<summary>Runs when a X fails</summary>
///<param name="objArg">The job that attempted X</param>
//********************************************************
private void HandleXNotSuccess(object objArg)
{
    // indicate "not busy"
    this.Cursor = Cursors.Arrow;

    // handle failure to do X
    …
}
```

Figure 2.8: Jobs and their derivations (Code: `WinAppInfrastruc`
`ture.Job.cs`)

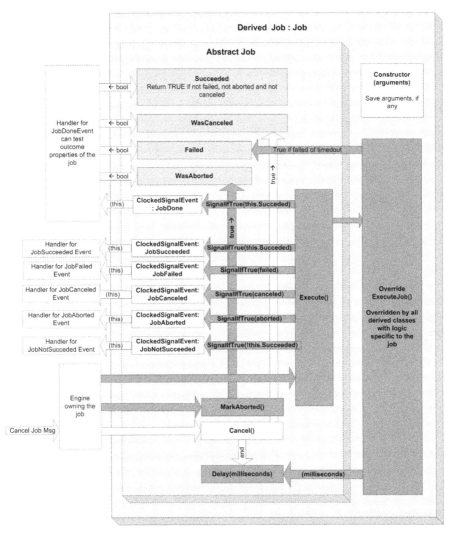

Use of jobs by other jobs or other code running in child threads

The logic in one job can allocate and enqueue a job for another engine.
In this case, the code does not use the completion events of the job.
Instead, if it must know the outcome or just know that the job has
completed, the initiating code actually waits for the job to complete.
That is, it sleeps until awakened by the engine that executes that job
when that job is done.

To do this, the initiating code sends a message's to enqueue the job for the other engine, invoking the messages `RunAndWaitForDone` method. For example:

```
MothSetupFile objSetupFile = new MothSetupFile("C:\\MothSetup.txt");
ReadTextFileJob objReadJob = new ReadTextFileJob(objSetupFile);
objReadJob.RunAndWaitForDone(BusNode.BN_FILE_SYSTEM);
```

Method `objReadJob.RunAndWaitForDone` enqueues the job for execution by the specified engine and sleeps until notified that the job has finished. Upon waking, `RunAndWaitForDone` returns, and your code picks up at the next statement.

Canceled, aborted, and timeout

The processing of every job that gets started eventually comes to an end. It may end because it has successfully completed its work, in failure because something went wrong or timed-out, or because it got notification to cancel what it is doing. If some logic needs to know when a job is done, it can count on notification. You must write your jobs so this is true.

Aborted jobs are jobs that get purged from an engine's queue and marked "aborted" before being taken up by the engine. In other words, the job never even begins to execute. This happens when an engine is killed with jobs still in its queue. If some logic in the program is expecting a notification upon completion of those jobs, it must get notification when jobs are aborted. Logic in the `Job` base class handles this. Code that discards a job without running it calls the job object's `MarkAborted` method. This will result in the firing of the `JobAborted` event in addition to the `JobDone` and `JobNotSucceeded` events.

Canceling a job is a little different. An engine will handle a message from elsewhere in the program to cancel the currently running job. It invokes the `Cancel` method of the current job. That method ends any delays that may be underway at that time and sets an internal cancel flag. The processing logic in the job's `ExecuteJob` method must periodically check that flag and, if found set, clean up and exit. The base class's

`Execute` method will then raise the `JobCanceled` event, in addition to the `JobDone` and `JobNotSucceeded` events.

Timeout is another issue. There is no mechanism in the FBW architecture, outside of a job object itself, for judging that a job has taken too long to complete its processing. If taking too long is a possibility, logic in a job's `ExecuteJob()` method is responsible for making that decision and abandoning the effort. As an example, after sending a command to an external device, the logic may wait only so long for a response. The job records a timeout as a failure, leading to the occurrence of the `JobDone`, `JobNotSucceeded`, and `JobFailed` events.

Delaying

The base class for jobs includes a protected method that is useful for producing delays in the processing done by a job. Invoke `base.Delay(milliseconds)` within your processing to sleep the given number of milliseconds. If `Delay` returns FALSE, it means your job has been canceled or the program is shutting down, and the job should abandon its work.

2.7 FBW Initialization and Program Shutdown

WinAppInfrastructure exposes a singleton class, `WinAppProgram Control,` with methods that initialize the FBW infrastructure and support an orderly shutdown of it for a program that is exiting.

The method `WinAppProgramControl.InitializeWinAppInfras tructure` must be called from the GUI thread before attempting to use any FBW feature.

A program that is closing must communicate that fact to all of its threads so that they can die. Otherwise, the program will hang and not fully close. The closing program calls

WinAppProgramControl.ShutDown for this purpose. That method sets a static property, ShuttingDown, which any code anywhere in the program can safely test at any time. Threads that find the ShuttingDown property TRUE, must abandon their processing and exit. The messages processing loops of engines (Section 2.6) continually test this flag and exit when it is TRUE.

The logic in ExecuteJob of every job must periodically check the flag and cease processing if it is set. Note that the Delay method in the Job base class makes this check and Delay returns FALSE if the program is shutting down.

To illustrate, the following code tests the flag on every iteration of a loop:

```
// keep processing until program shutting down
while (!WinAppProgramControl.ShuttingDown)
{
    new  DebugMsg("Not shutdown yet").Send();
    base.Delay(1000);
}
```

Typically the FormClosed event of the program's main form will invoke WinAppProgramControl.ShuttingDown as the program begins to exit.

Figure 2.9: Support for initializing and starting FBW operation and for orderly shutdown (Code: `WinAppInfrastructure.WinAppProgramControl`)

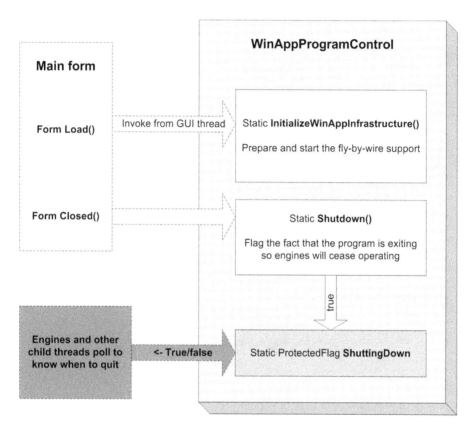

Chapter 3: FBW Aids

This chapter presents a number of classes that simplify the interface to certain GUI controls and aid in timing activity.

3.1 Fly-By-Wire Buttons

Rather than directly wire button controls into your forms, you can give the buttons a presence on the logical bus by wrapping the buttons in instances of the `FBWButton` class and deal with them using logical messages.

Figure 3.1 illustrates the technique. Your program allocates a bus node for a button and gives the bus node and the button control to an instance of `FBWButton`. Then link a message handler for the `ButtonClickMsg` sent by the bus node assigned to the button.

`WinAppInfrastructure` provides additional messages for controlling the button. To enable or disable the button, send it a `ButtonEnableMsg`. To change its caption (label), send it a `ButtonTextMsg` with the new caption as its payload. To hide the button or make it visible, send a `ButtonVisibleMsg` with a payload of FALSE or TRUE.

Figure 3.1: The FBWButton class wraps a button control to give it a presence on the logical bus. (Code: `WinAppInfrastructure.FBWButton.cs`)

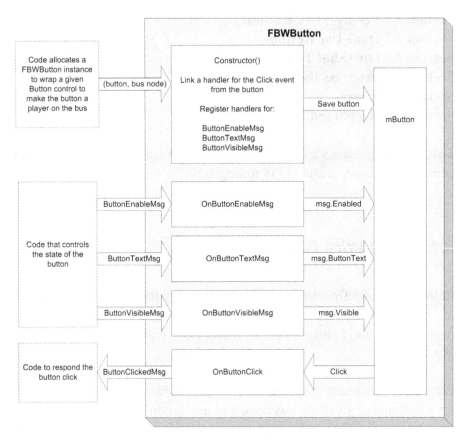

3.2 Dual-Use Buttons

GUIs often use a single button for two things. The button's use may toggle between Start and Stop, or Open and Close, for example. When clicking the button will start something, the button's label reads "Start"; when clicking the button will stop something, the button's label reads "Stop."

Because the button generates the same event when clicked regardless of which action it is currently configured to initiate (Start or Stop), the handler for that event generally has to look into what the button is currently configured to do and include branches for each case. Or you can derive a StartStopButton class from DualUseFBWButton (Figure 3.2) to help simplify this logic.

Allocate an instance of StartStopButton, passing its constructor the button control to manage. Then link different message handlers for instances of ButtonClickedMsg from each of the two bus nodes in use by the dual-use button. One handler will run when the user clicks the button while it is showing its initial caption ("Start"); the other handler runs when the user clicks the button while it is showing its alternative caption ("Stop").

Classes like StartStopButton class derive from an abstract base class, DualUseFBWButton. The base does all the work. The derived classes merely furnish the initial and alternate captions for the button and the bus nodes for the two uses.

When a user clicks a button that is under management by a DualUseButton class, that sends a ButtonClickedMsg from the bus node corresponding to its current use and disables the button

But it does not automatically toggle the button caption because we won't want the alternate label to show until the action initiated by the click completes successfully. When the action completes, code carrying it out sends a ButtonEnableMsg to the bus node assigned to the alternative use of the button if the action succeeded.

That handler for that message in the DualUseButton object changes the caption of the button to show its alternative caption, rewires the object to send the ButtonClickedMsg from the alternative node on the next button click, and possibly re-enables the button.

If the action failed, code performing it may choose to leave the button showing the initial caption and re-enable the button or leave it disabled.

As illustration, the following code sets up one method to handle clicks when the button is labeled "Start" and a different method for clicks when the button label reads "Stop."

Figure 3.2: `DualUseFBWButton` extended to manage a Start/Stop button (Code: `WinAppInfrastructure.DualUseFBWButton.cs`)

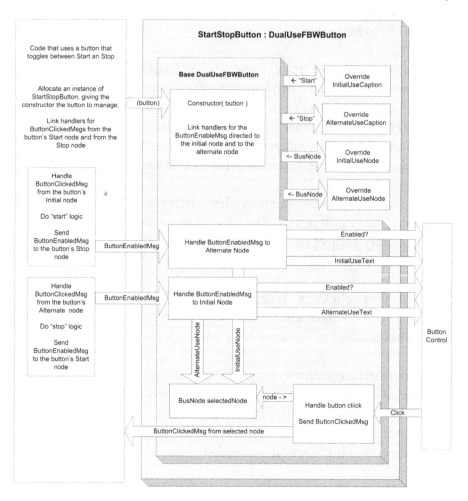

3.3 One-Shot Timers

A `OneShotTimer` is useful for giving notification of elapsed time in the GET (Figure 3.3). Allocate an instance of `OneShotTimer`, link handlers to its `TimerExpiredEvent` and `TimerCanceledEvent`, and invoke its `StartTimer` method passing it a number of milliseconds. When the given number of milliseconds have passed, the timer fires its `TimerExpiredEvent`, and the handler you linked to it runs in the GET. In accord with its name, a `OneShotTimer` fires one time. To use it again, you must invoke its `StartTimer` method again.

Should code decide to cancel the timing, it invokes the `StopTimer` method of the timer. That will cause the timer's `TimerCanceledEvent` to fire and the handler you linked to it will run in the GET.

For illustration:

```
// prepare a timer to support progress
private  OneShotTimer  mobjProgressTimer
this.mobjProgressTimer = new OneShotTimer();
this.mobjProgressTimer.TimerExpiredEvent.LinkHandler(
this.OnTimerExpiredEvent);

// start timing - expires in 1 sec
this.mobjProgressTimer.StartTimer(1000);

// stop the timer before it has run to expiration
this.mobjProgressTimer.StopTimer();

// runs in the GET when the timer expires
private void OnTimerExpiredEvent(object objArg)
  {
     OneShotTimer objTimer = (OneShotTimer) objArg;
     ….

     // start the timer again if want to go again...
     objTimer.StartTimer(1000);
  }

// runs in the GET if the timer is stopped before expiring
private void OnTimerCanceledEvent(object objArg)
  {
     OneShotTimer objTimer = (OneShotTimer) objArg;
     ….
  }
```

Figure 3.3: OneShotTimer gives notification in the GET after a given time. (Code: WinAppInfrastructure.OneShotTimer.cs)

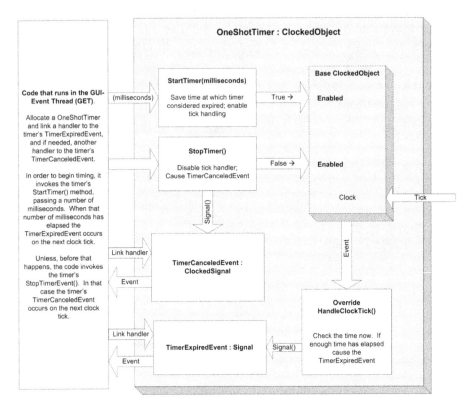

3.4 Progress Bar Manager

An instance of ProgressBarManager (Figure 3.4) coordinates the display of progress in a progress bar control and associated label control on a GUI form or user control. Code that allocates an instance of ProgressBarManager gives it a progress bar control and label control to manage and a bus node to distinguish those controls from other pairs of progress bar and label controls. Code anywhere in the program can use these controls to display progress by sending certain messages to the bus node assigned to the progress bar.

A `ProgressBarManager` links its handlers for several progress-related messages:

- `ProgressBarSetMaxProgressMsg` – Payload is the maximum value to set in the progress bar (i.e., define what is 100 percent)
- `ProgressBarUpdateProgressMsg` – Payload is increment to add to the current progress value.
- `ProgressBarSetProgressMsg` – Payload is the value to set as the current progress value.
- `ProgressBarClearProgressMsg` – Reset progress.
- `ProgressBarStartAutoProgressMsg` – Start auto-progress.

The `ProgressBarManager` *class* has five static methods that will form and send these messages for you if you invoke them:

- `ProgressBarManager.SetMaxForProgressBar(bus node, progress-maximum)`
- `ProgressBarManager.UpdateProgressBarProgress(bus node, progress-increment)`
- `ProgressBarManager.SetProgressBarProgress(bus node, progress-value)`
- `ProgressBarManager.ClearProgressBar(bus node)`
- `ProgressBarManager.StartAutoProgress(bus node, max seconds)`

Augmented Progress

When a component of the program can quantify how much it has to do before beginning, it can show augmented progress. It begins by calling `SetMaxForProgressBar` to establish the maximum value for the progress bar. As it makes progress through its work, the component repeatedly invokes `UpdateProgressBarProgress` or `SetProgressBarProgress`. The former sends a message bearing a value that the recipient adds to the current progress value. The latter sends a message bearing a value that the recipient assigns as the current progress.

The handlers for the messages update the current progress value of the progress bar. The new current progress value will be some percentage of the maximum value set by the `ProgressBarSetMaxProgressMsg`; the message handlers calculate that percentage and display it in the label control.

Auto Progress

When a component of the program cannot quantify how much it has to do before beginning, it uses the auto-progress feature of `ProgressBarManager`. It makes an assumption about how long the work could take, worst case. Say it is N seconds. The component then invokes `ProgressBarManager.StartAutoProgress(bus node, N)`.

`ProgressBarManager` wires itself to run a method in the GET once every second. That method advances the display of progress, one-Nth of the total progress displayable, every second. When the component that initiated auto-progress determines that the activity is complete, or has timed out, it invokes `ProgressBarManager.ClearProgressBar(bus node)`.

That methods sends a `ProgressBarClearProgressMsg` to the given bus node. The handler for that message clears the progress display and stops the `OneShotTimer` that was giving it events every second.

Figure 3.4: Progress Bar Manager coordinates the display of progress on a form or user control. (Code: `Winappinfrastructure.ProgressBarManager.cs`)

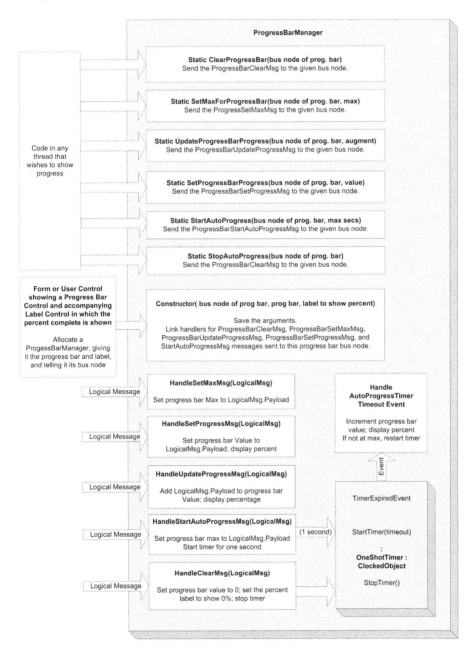

3.5 Timer

Logic running in child threads frequently needs the ability to time its activity. WinAppInfrastructure provides a utility class (Figure 3.5) to meet that need.

Figure 3.5: Instances of `WinAppTimer` enable child threads to easily time their activity.
(Code: `Winappinfrastructure.WinAppTimer.cs`)

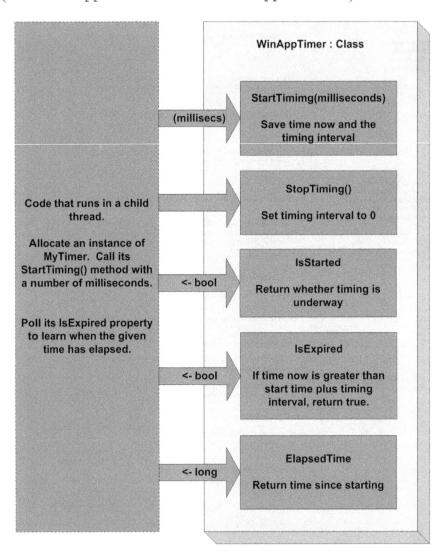

`WinAppTimer` is intended for use by child threads because its properties are polled. Allocate an instance of `WinAppTimer` and invoke its `StartTiming` method to begin timing. Periodically test its `IsExpired` property to learn when the time has elapsed. While timing is underway, a timer's `ElapsedTime` property gives the number of milliseconds that have passed since the invocation of `StartTiming`.

For illustration, the following code prints a debug message every second for ten seconds:

```
WinAppTimer objTimer = new WinAppTimer();
objTimer.StartTiming(10000);

// do until timer expires...
while(!objTimer.IsExpired)
{
    string strTime = objTimer.ElapsedTime.ToString();
    new DebugMsg("Time: " + strTime).Send();
    this.Delay(1000);
}
```

3.6 Registered Message Handlers

Code that registers message handlers must remove the registrations before the code can go completely out of scope and be disposed. To help manage these functions, WinAppInfrastructure furnishes the class `RegisteredMessageHandlers`. An instance of it remembers the handlers that are registered on behalf of the code that allocated it, so that, with the invocation of one of its methods, it can remove all the registrations without the possibility of forgetting some.

For example, this code registers handlers for two types of messages directed to a given bus node:

```
// link handlers for message to show and clear the text that
// describes what the bar is showing progress of

private RegisteredMessageHandlers mobjMsgHandlers;
mobjMsgHandlers = new RegisteredMessageHandlers(enmBusNode);
mobjMsgHandlers.RegisterHandler(typeof(LabelProgressMsg),
this.HandleLabelProgressMsg);

mobjMsgHandlers.RegisterHandler(typeof(ClearProgressLabelMsg),
this.HandleClearProgressLabel);
```

And this code removes the registrations:

```
mobjMsgHandlers.RemoveHandlers();
```

Forms that process messages typically register message handlers in their `FormLoad` methods and remove the registrations in their `FormClosing` methods. Unless they remove the registrations, their message-handling methods will continue to be invoked even though the form is closed.

Figure 3.6: Instances of `RegisteredMessageHandlers` manage the registration and removal of message handlers on behalf of the code that needs to remove all its handler registrations in order to go completely out of scope. (Code: `WinAppInfrastructure.` `RegisteredMessageHandlers.cs`)

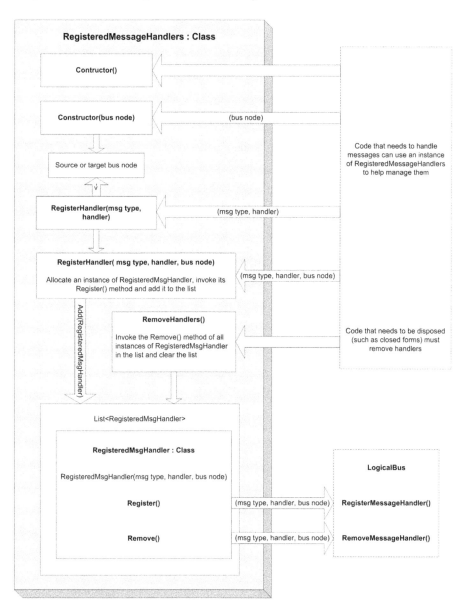

Chapter 4: FBWwinAppDemo –
Design Principles

In the next chapter, we will put it all together in a complete demonstration Windows application, prosaically named FBW*winAppDemo*. To make it interesting, FBWwinAppDemo controls a robot. The robot follows a source of infrared radiation (such as a person) around the room, seemingly attracted to the IR source like a moth to a flame. We'll call the robot *MOTH*.

But first, let's specify the behavior of the robot and set forth some guidelines and design principles for its controlling program.

4.1 Design Goals

Picture a small platform with four wheels. The platform supports a battery and a PC running Windows. Motors with embedded controllers drive the wheels using power from the battery, under direction of FBWwinAppDemo executing on the PC. The final component of MOTH is an array of infrared radiation (IR) sensors, arranged in a horizontal arc, pointing in the direction the robot can roll.

Figure I.1 (in the Introduction) shows FBWwinAppDemo in context. Each wheel controller receives commands—text strings—through an RS232 serial port. FBWwinAppDemo communicates with the motor controllers through four COM ports. The application periodically samples input from the IR sensors.

When there is no IR present, the program commands all of the wheels to stop. When IR input indicates that a source of IR, a person, say, is directly in front, FBWwinAppDemo commands all of the wheels to run at normal speed, and the robot advances on the person.

When a person is located to the right-front of the robot, sensors report that IR predominates on the right; FBWwinAppDemo commands wheels on the right to run slowly and wheels on the left to turn at normal speed. MOTH turns right. As it does (and assuming the IR source remains stationary) the robot soon is facing the person again. At that time, input from the sensors shows the source to be directly in front, so FBWwinAppDemo commands all the wheels to rotate at normal speed, and the robot is again advancing toward the person.

Now, suppose the person moves to the left of MOTH. FBWwinAppDemo then sees IR predominately on the left; it tells the left wheels to rotate slowly. The robot turns left and is soon again facing the source. The program then tells all the wheels to rotate at normal speed, and MOTH rolls on toward the person.

The previous chapters of this book gave us the building blocks for a fly-by-wire program. In the next chapter we will begin to assemble those blocks into a working Windows application. But first, consider some principles of software design.

4.2 Unconditional Programmi5ng

MOTH is a simpler version of *Genghis*, a robot built by MIT professor Rodney Brooks and his graduate students. In his book *Flesh and Machines*, professor Brooks describes his creation. Genghis looks like a large insect with six legs and an array of IR sensors on its "face." When switched on, it will chase a person around a room. It scrambles over obstacles, apparently intent on catching its "prey."

But in the software that animates the robot, there is no place that represents "any intent to follow something, or any goal to reach it."

This is true of FBWwinAppDemo also. Its deceivingly purposeful behavior arises from the reflexive interplay of interconnected objects tied to the sensors and actuators of the robot.

The program is spinal, not cerebral. It reacts; it doesn't think. It is reflexive, not contemplative. The programmer does the thinking before the application ever runs, anticipating and accommodating contingency in its design so that the running program itself need sense and respond to contingency as little as possible. At as few places as possible in the execution of the code should it have to ask itself, "Why am I here?" "Should I do this, or should I do that?" Mostly blind reflex is what you want.

We will see this in FBWwinAppDemo. Figure 5.1 depicts its GUI main form. Among other things, the program disables buttons on the GUI whenever clicks on them would initiate something that is out of line at that time. When the state of the program changes to make those actions appropriate, the buttons become enabled. Consequently, code to handle button clicks never has to ask itself, "Is now a good time to do this?" It must be a good time; otherwise, the click event would not have occurred.

Furthermore, click-handling code doesn't think about what to do. The code behind a given button does the same thing every time. Generally, what it does includes sending a message to enqueue a job for execution by a given engine or a message to cancel a currently executing job. But there are no if-statements, no branches. Whatever contingency is inherent in this activity was resolved by other code, resulting in "wiring" of the program (in this case an enabled or disabled button) that is appropriate for its current state.

A dual-use button (Chapter 3) is an even better example. The `Start` button on the GUI of FBWwinAppDemo (Figure 5.1) is such a button. The program uses the same button to start MOTH's operation and to stop it. A click on the button while its label reads "Start" starts operation; a click on the button while its label reads "Stop" stops operation. How can this be achieved without an if-statement?

The program employs an instance of `DualUseFBWButton` to manage the Start/Stop button. A `DualUseFBWButton` object sends a message from one bus node when a click occurs while the button shows an initial label ("Start" in this case), and it sends a message from another bus node while the button shows an alternate label ("Stop" in this case). The program links different handlers for the messages from the different nodes. One handler does what is needed to "start," then prepares the `DualUseFBWButton` to function in the alternate role, that is, "stop." If a user clicks the button while the button is prepared for the alternate role, a message from the alternate bus node is sent, and the handler for that message runs the "stop" logic.

Another good example is the way the wheel engines are wired differently to function as right-wheel or left-wheel controllers. The two left-wheel engines are instances of class `LeftWheel`, and the two for the right wheels are instances of `RightWheel`. `LeftWheel` and `RightWheel` derive from class `Wheel`, but they differ in how they handle messages announcing the direction of the IR source. An instance of `LeftWheel` connects IR-mostly-on-the-left messages to logic that commands its wheel to turn slowly. It connects IR-mostly-on-the-right messages to logic that commands its wheel to turn quickly. Instances of `RightWheel` do exactly the reverse. So with no thought of coordinating their efforts, the wheels on the left and right run at speeds that turn MOTH toward the source of the IR. The thought that produced the coordination was done by the designer.

Thus, the program allocates instances of classes, animates them with the settings that fix each instance's internal wiring, and deploys them, hooking the outputs of some to the inputs of others like synapses in a brain. This style of programming requires very little branching, very few if-statements, so I call it "unconditional programming."

4.3 Need to Know

Most of the program adopts an epistemology of revelation and faith: it believes and acts upon what it is told. *A priori* knowledge—

miscellaneous, arbitrary information from realms outside the program— is not scattered around the program but localized and made available on a need-to-know basis.

An example of *a priori* knowledge is the fact that the commands to make a wheel turn at different speeds are "Speed=Slow," "Speed=Fast," and "Speed=Stop." FBWwinAppDemo embeds this knowledge in one place.

Moreover, one piece of code forms speed commands, and it knows to add the prefix "Speed=" to one of these speeds and to append a new-line character to make a speed control command. If new versions of the motor controllers look for a different format of speed commands, the programmer adapts the program to the change with a modification in one place.

4.4 State Machines

Probably a reliable program of any complexity must be a *state-machine*. A state-machine is a logical regimen. It imposes order on a complex set of interactions by making everything deterministic.

A state-machine is always in a well-defined state. It is never partly in one state and partly in another. Three things characterize a state: 1) what can be done in it; 2) how it can be exited; and 3) which other states can be reached from it.

An example of a state-machine is a business meeting run by Robert's Rules of Order. Such a meeting is always in some state, and in each state only certain things are in order. Sometimes a motion to close debate, say, is acceptable and sometimes not. The steps for moving the meeting from debating a motion to voting on it are defined.

The chairman of the business meeting keeps track of the state of the meeting, which allows him to rule on the propriety of statements or requests from the floor.

In the typical state-machine program, the analogous knowledge resides in a *state-variable*. The state-variable holds a value that represents the state of the program at any given moment. If there are five possible states, the state-variable will, at various times, contain *0*, *1*, *2*, *3*, and *4*. The program might examine the value of the state-variable in order to know what to do.

Unfortunately, this technique invites the program to engage in an interior monologue of the sort we'd like to avoid: "What state am I in?" "May I do this now?" "May I transition to that new state?" The ideal program eliminates the state-variable altogether and allows the state to be implicit. The program disseminates the effect of a state change *at the moment the transition occurs* and doesn't look back. The effect of the state change is to rewire the program, to cast it into a new posture for new circumstances. The sum of the capabilities of the new posture *is* the state.

The chairman of the business meeting could likewise dispense with remembering the "state" of the meeting—if, at the moment of state transition, he could disable in everyone present the ability to initiate anything out of order in the new state.

4.5 Elegance in Program Design

Describing the Standard Model of elementary particle physics, theoretical physicist Steven Weinberg wrote, "We still have too many arbitrary features" in the model. It has eighteen numerical quantities, whose values are known from experiment, but "we don't know why nature chooses those values; any theory with 18 free parameters is too arbitrary to be satisfactory."

If this is how aesthetics enters into particle physics, that discipline has something in common with computer programming. Even though most of my work answers real needs in the real world, computer programming has enduring interest for me only as an art form. I'm not talking about how the program looks to users, the artistic aspects of the appearance of the GUI. I'm thinking of how it all works on the inside, how it is coded.

There are always many ways to structure and code a program that will achieve the goals for it. Some ways are brutal and some elegant. What constitutes beauty in a computer program? The previous sections suggest the qualities of a Windows app that render it elegant in my eyes.

The elegant application is reflexive, not contemplative. It does not attempt to represent intention or think of itself as waiting for something. It is composed mostly of event handlers. The events have very narrow meaning so that code in the handlers is without branches, without if-statements. If, at the margin, the program must poll for something, it devotes a child thread to do the polling and to convey what it finds using events.

The elegant application is a state-machine in which the state is implicit in the current wiring of the program. The program disseminates the effect of a state change at the moment the transition occurs by rewiring the program. The sum of the capabilities of the rewired program is the new state.

The elegant application isolates *a priori* knowledge and promulgates it from a single spot. You have a beautiful program when you can replace a miscellaneous fact with another, and the effect of the change ripples through the program without requiring any changes to the code beyond that needed to embody the fact in the program at one place.

Speaking metaphorically and mathematically, the program spans the space created for it by the requirements, using the minimum set of mutually orthogonal components. It is a mesh of simple interconnections that is without awareness or a sense of the future between events. As such it settles a static solution onto an inherently dynamic problem, in much the same way that the space–time continuum of special relativity achieves a depiction of the past, present, and future that eliminates the dynamism of time.

Chapter 5: FBWwinAppDemo – Design

Look again at Figure I.1 in the introduction. The darker box in the center of that diagram represents the FBWwinAppDemo program in context. As appropriate for a context diagram, it is empty, just one of the components of the system. This chapter takes us from that empty box to the application's completed design as depicted in Figure I.2.

5.1 What Can You Do for Me?

The context diagram shows us what we have to work with: a collection of eight infrared radiation sensors, four wheel controllers and wheel-setup files. These entities appear on the architecture drawing in dashed outline to indicate they are outside the program. FBWwinAppDemo gets to think of them as black boxes that manage certain details for it. Let's understand what they bring to the party.

Wheel Controllers

A wheel controller comprises a motor and embedded processor. It can hold its wheel stopped, turn it slowly, or turn it rapidly. Wheel controllers accept the following commands as new-line-terminated text strings through a serial port:

Speed=Stop   Stop the wheel

Speed=Slow   Turn the wheel slowly

Speed=Fast   Turn the wheel rapidly

SelfTest   Perform self-test and within ten seconds reply OK or FAILED

PARAMx=<value>   Adopt <value> for wheel control parameter x; reply ACK or NAK

Wheel controllers append a new-line character to their responses to PARAMx commands and the SelfTest command. They operate with communication settings of 19200 baud, eight data bits, one stop bit, and no parity.

If a wheel controller does not receive a Speed command for 500 milliseconds, it stops its wheel.

IR Sensors

MOTH's "eyes" consist of a bank of eight IR sensors with a USB interface to the PC. The output of a sensor is a value from *0* to *1023*, which is proportional to the intensity of infrared radiation registered by the sensor.

We imagine that the manufacturer furnishes a C# library with a class— SensorBank—that serves as an API to the sensors. An instance of SensorBank has the following methods:

- LatchReadings reads and saves a reading from each sensor. It takes up to ten milliseconds to complete the readings.

- GetReading(intChannel) furnishes the latest reading from the given A/D channel, i.e., from a given sensor.

Wheel Setup Files

These files may reside anywhere in the Windows file system. They contain PARAMx commands, that, when downloaded to wheel controllers, tune their operation in some way. For example, the value for PARAM0 may define RPM for slow wheel rotation, and PARAM1 may define RPM for rapid wheel rotation.

There may be any number of these files, but when a user picks one to download, the contents of that file go to all the wheel controllers.

5.2 Constructing FBWwinAppDemo

Again, Figure I.2 is a diagram of the application's fly-by-wire architecture. The components of the program communicate over a logical bus using logical messages. Moreover, no component is in charge. True, code runs as the program loads to create and initialize the other components, but that code is transient and does not continue to control operation after setting it in motion.

The following sections describe the components of FBWwinAppDemo as seen in the architecture diagram.

Main Form

Figure 5.1 depicts the program's main form as it appears while the robot is tracking an IR source that is somewhat to its left. It shows readings from the IR sensors, the outcome of self-testing for each wheel, and the last speed command sent to each wheel. There are buttons for initiating wheel self-testing, downloading of setup files to the wheel controllers, starting and stopping the IR source tracking, and closing the program. All the buttons are snapped onto the logical bus using FBWButton wrappers. A progress bar, snapped onto the logical bus by means of an instance of ProgressBarManager, shows progress during self-testing and download.

Table 5.5 details the controls on this form and their use. In general, all the information appearing on this form comes to it as the payload of messages. Clicks on any of the buttons create and queue jobs for engines.

Figure 5.1: FBWwinAppDemo's Main Form showing raw IR readings and wheel-speed commands (Code: `RobotController.frmMothMain.cs`)

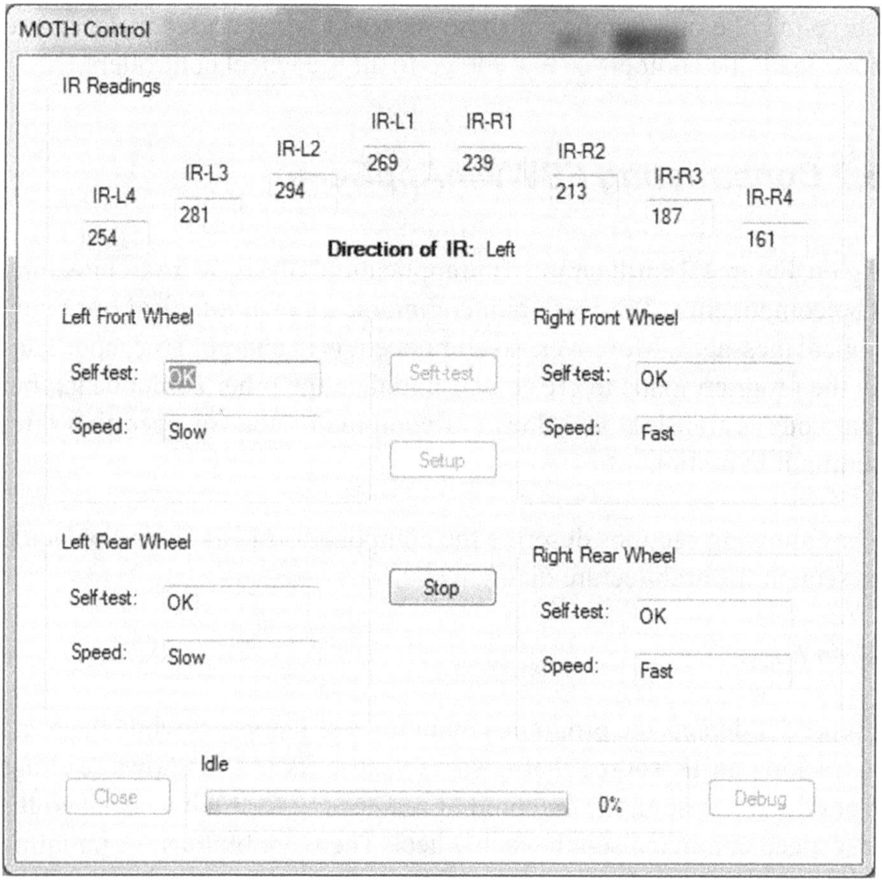

InfraredSensors Engine

This engine executes a `MonitorIRJob` that periodically samples the readings of IR registered by the sensors. It sends logical messages reporting the raw readings, messages to report that no IR source is present, or that the IR source is centered in front of MOTH or to the left-front or right-front. Figure 5.2 illustrates `InfraredSensors` and `MonitorIRJob`.

Figure 5.2: The `InfraredSensors` engine sends IR direction messages that the wheel engines use to control wheels. (Code: `RobotController.InfraredSensors.cs`)

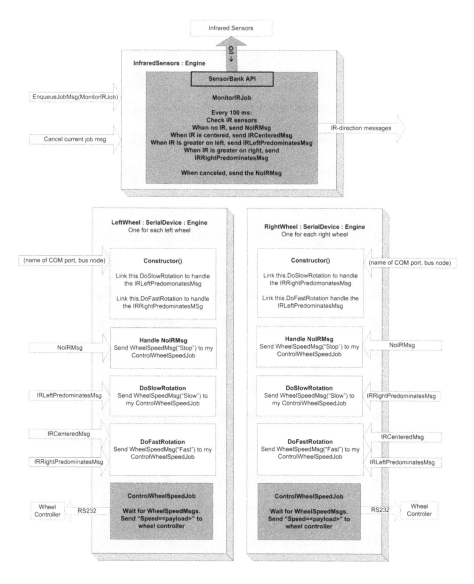

Wheel Engines

Two instances of LeftWheel engine represent and control the left wheels, and two instances of RightWheel engine represent and control the right wheels. The only difference between left-wheel and right-wheel engines is how they respond to messages that indicate the direction of the IR source.

A LeftWheel engine wires IRLeftPredominatesMsgs to a handler that commands its wheel to turn slowly, and wires IRRightPredominatesMsgs to a handler that commands its wheel to turn rapidly. The RightWheel engines do the reverse. The combination of these behaviors causes the robot to turn left when IR predominates on the left, and to turn right when the IR predominates on the right.

While tracking an IR source, each wheel engine executes a `ControlWheelSpeedJob`. The job waits for wheel-speed messages. Other parts of `Wheel` receive IR-direction messages from `InfraredSensors` in the GUI-Event Thread and respond by sending wheel-speed messages to their own instance of `ControlWheelSpeedJob`. The payload of wheel-speed messages is either "Stop," "Slow," or "Fast." `ControlWheelSpeedJob` turns a speed into a speed command and sends it to its wheel controller. Then it waits for another wheel-speed message. Figure 5.2 suggests the interaction between the `InfraredSensors` and wheel engines.

When MOTH is not looking for or tracking an IR source, an instance of `Wheel` can execute a job to initiate self-testing by the wheel controller, await the result, and announce the result in a message. Wheel engines will also execute jobs to download setup information to their wheel controllers.

File System

WinAppInfrastructure furnishes this engine. It manages file system I/O. In FBWwinAppDemo, it executes jobs `ReadTextFileJob` and `AppendToTextFileJob`. From time-to-time, file I/O can be slow, but FBWwinAppDemo is nevertheless well behaved because it kicks responsibility for the sometimes sluggish file I/O up to an engine, a child thread. There it can take as long as it needs to without affecting the program's ability to repaint or attend to the other balls it has in the air.

Error Engine

WinAppInfrastructure furnishes the `ErrorEngine`. It uses a child thread to display error messages so that other processing can continue while waiting for a user to acknowledge the message. The engine displays error message windows in such a way that they stay topmost on the desktop until closed by the user.

Debug Forms

Debug Forms is the final component depicted in the architecture diagram for FBWwinAppDemo. This refers to two forms supplied by WinAppInfrastructure and one by the FBWwinAppDemo project that aid a programmer in debugging the application. The first form can display any logical message seen on the logical bus, that is, any message sent by any component of the program. The second shows the current status of any engine or job. The third form interacts with a user to simulate IR input and responses from wheel controllers so that FBWwinAppDemo can run and be debugged even before hardware is available.

Section 5.11 describes these forms and their use.

5.3 FBWwinAppDemo States

FBWwinAppDemo is a state-machine, but there is no place that records the state or checks it to decide how to behave. The state at any given moment is implicit in how the program is wired and in the jobs that are running at that time.

Table 5.1 lists the states that the FBWwinAppDemo inhabits and defines what is true in each state. Figure 5.3 is a state transition diagram for the program showing which states are reachable from which other states and the transition triggers.

Table 5.1: FBWwinAppDemo's States

State	Jobs Running	Buttons enabled	Cursor	Progress Bar label
INITIALIZING	None	None	App-Starting	Idle
UNTESTED `MothStateUntested.cs`	None	Self-Test, Close	Arrow	Idle
SELFTESTING `MothStateSelftesting.cs`	`SelfTestWheelJob` by all wheel engines	None	Hourglass	Self-testing
UNCONFIGURED `MothStateUnconfigured.cs`	None	Self-Test, Setup, Close	Arrow	Idle
DOWNLOADING `MothStateDownloading.cs`	`DownloadWheelSetup-Job` by all wheel engines	Close	Hourglass	Down-loading...
STOPPED `MothStateStopped.cs`	None	Start/ Stop, Self-Test, Setup, Close	Arrow	
RUNNING `MothStateRunning.cs`	`MonitorIRJob` by `InfraredSensors` engine `ControlWheelSpeedJob` by all wheel engine...	Start/ Stop as Stop	Arrow-Hourglass	Idle

	None	N/A	N/A	Idle
DEBILITATED `MothStateDebilitated.cs`				
CLOSING `MothStateClosing.cs`	None	N/A	N/A	Idle

The code employs classes to encapsulate the logic for rewiring the program to function in a given state. Figure 5.4 depicts the logic for wiring the program for the state in which the program is controlling the robot, the RUNNING state.

Abstract base class `MothState` includes virtual properties to hold defaults for the states of the buttons (enabled or not), the cursor shown by the main form, and which node is selected for the Start/Stop button in a given state. Classes derived from `MothState` to represent the states of the program override these properties with values that combine to define a real state of the program.

As shown in the figure, class `MothStateRunning` derives from the abstract base class `MothState`. Its constructor hooks an instance of the class to come into play when a user clicks the Start/Stop button while it is configured to function as the Start button. A click on that button at that time leads to an invocation of method `EnterMothState()` in the derived class.

That method invokes the corresponding method in the base class to send the messages that set the states of the buttons and the progress bar and determines which cursor appears for the main form; this achieves the basic wiring of the program for the RUNNING state. Method `EnterMothState()` in `MothStateRunning` completes the wiring by starting the jobs that carry the burden of execution in the RUNNING state.

Figure 5.3: State Transition Diagram

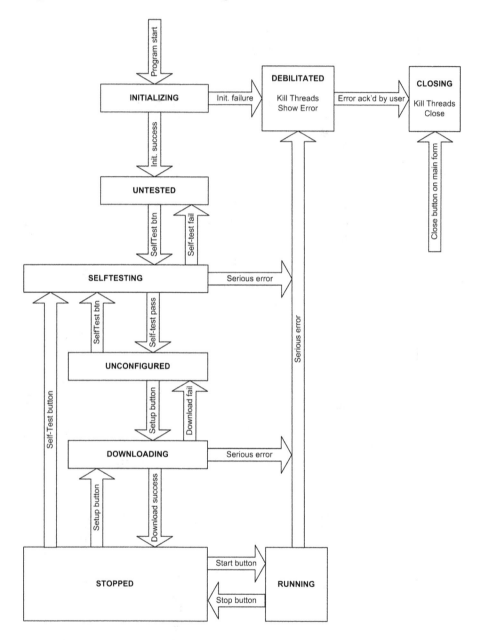

Figure 5.4 State-definition class `MothStateRunning` derives from `MothState` to embody the logic to wire the program to function in the RUNNING state.

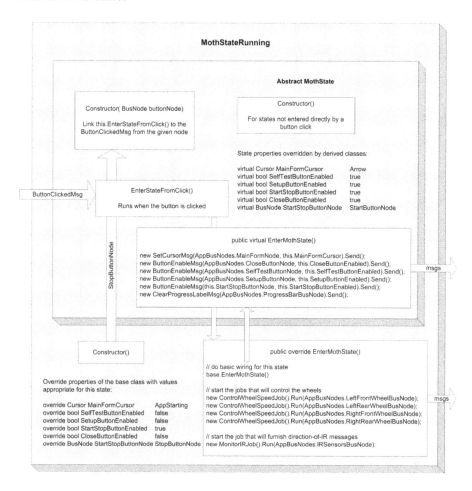

5.4 Jobs

FBWwinAppDemo does its work using engines that execute jobs. Table 5.2 lists and describes the jobs.

Table 5.2: Jobs employed by FBWwinAppDemo

Job Name	Executing Engine	Runs in States	Description
MonitorIRJob	InfraredSensors	RUNNING	Periodically read IR sensors and send messages NoIRMsg, IRCenteredMsg, IRLeftPredominatesMsg, IRRightPredominatesMsg, IRReadingsMsg
ControlWheel-SpeedJob	All wheel engines	RUNNING	Wait for instances of WheelSpeedMsg, form their payloads into speed control commands and send the commands to the wheel controller
SelfTestWheelJob	All wheel engines	SELFTESTING	Send the wheel controller the command to self-test; wait for the response, and send a WheelSelfTestResultsMsg bearing the results as its payload
DownloadWheel-SetupJob	All wheel engines	DOWNLOADING	Read in the contents of a setup file of a given name; send its lines to the wheel, updating progress bar after each line
ReadTextFileJob	WinAppFileSystem	DOWNLOADING	Read the contents of a setup text file of a given name
AppendTo-TextFileJob	WinAppFileSystem	Potentially any	Append a line of text to a file of a given name
ShowErrorJob	ErrorEngine	Potentially any	Show error message forms

5.5 Bus Nodes

The major components in FBWwinAppDemo send and receive messages. Some messages identify their senders. Some identify their intended recipient. Others have such a narrow meaning that the source is implicit, and any node that cares to can make itself the recipient of all messages of that type. Table 5.3 lists the bus nodes used by FBWwinAppDemo.

Table 5.3: Bus Nodes in FBWwinAppDemo

Bus Node ID	Use
BN_NONE	To initialize a `BusNode` variable until actual node assigned
BN_ANYNODE	Implies message source implicit and recipient can by any node
BN_FILE_SYSTEM	Identifies the File System engine
BN_ERROR_ENGINE	Identifies the Error Engine
BN_DEBUG_BUTTON	Identifies the button used to launch the Debug form
BN_DEBUG_FORM	Identifies the Debug form
BN_APPL_1	Identifies the Progress Bar on the Main form
BN_APPL_2	Identifies the Infrared Sensors engine
BN_APPL_3	Identifies the LF wheel engine
BN_APPL_4	Identifies the LR wheel engine
BN_APPL_5	Identifies the RF wheel engine
BN_APPL_6	Identifies the RR wheel engine
BN_APPL_7	Identifies the Self-test button
BN_APPL_8	Identifies the Setup button
BN_APPL_9	Identifies the Start/Stop button when used to Start
BN_APPL_10	Identifies the Start/Stop button when used to Stop
BN_APPL_11	Identifies the Close button
BN_APPL_12	Identifies the Main form

5.6 Logical Messages

The components of FBWwinAppDemo communicate using logic messages. Messages may identify the sender or the targeted receiver. They may bear a payload (any object) from the sender to the receiver.

5.7 Controls on the Main Form

FBWwinAppDemo's main (Figure 5.1) form mounts a number of standard controls and user controls. It is through these controls that a user interacts with the robot.

Table 5.4: Logical messages employed by FBWwinAppDemo

Message Name	Sender(s)	Receiver(s)	Payload
NoIRMsg	MonitorIRJob running in InfraredSensors engine	Wheel engines; uctlShowIR instances	None
IRCenteredMsg	MonitorIRJob running in InfraredSensors engine	Wheel engines; uctlShowIR instances	None
IRLeft-PredominatesMsg	MonitorIRJob running in InfraredSensors engine	Wheel engines; uctlShowIR instances	None
IRRight-PredominatesMsg	MonitorIRJob running in InfraredSensors engine	Wheel engines; uctlShowIR instances	None
IRReadingsMsg	MonitorIRJob running in InfraredSensors engine	uctlShowIR instances	Hashtable of raw IR readings keyed to A/D channels
WheelSpeedMsg	Wheel engine instances send them to their own jobs	ControlWheelSpeedJob running in wheel engines	"Stop" "Slow" "Fast"
WheelSelfTest-ResultsMsg	Wheel engines	Instances of uctlWheelMonitors	String sent by wheel controller
DebugMsg	Any code	DebugForm	Text
ShowAdditional-DebugMsg	DebugSupport	frmMothMain	None
ErrorMsg	Any code	ErrorEngine	WinAppError object

Message	Sender	Receiver	Value
`EnqueueJobMsg`	`frmMothMain` `DownloadWheelSetupJob`	**Wheel engines;** `InfraredSensors` **engine;** `ErrorEngine;` `FileSystem` **engine**	Job `object`
`CancelCurrent-` `JobMsg`	`frmMothMain`	**Wheel engines;** `InfraredSensors` **engine**	None
`EngineStatusMsg`	Base class of all engines	`frmEngineMonitor`	Text
`JobStatusMsg`	Base class of all engines	`frmEngineMonitor`	Text
`GetEngine-` `StatusMsg`	`frmEngineMonitor`	Base class of all engines	None
`ProgressBarClearMsg`	`frmMothMain` `DownloadWheelSetupJob`	`ProgressBarManager` for the `uctlProgressBar`	None
`ProgressBar-` `SetMaxMsg`	`DownloadWheelSetupJob`	`ProgressBarManager` for the `uctlProgressBar`	0 to max `int`
`ProgressBar-` `SetProgressMsg`	`DownloadWheelSetupJob`	`ProgressBarManager` for the `uctlProgressBar`	0 to max `int`
`LabelProgressMsg`	Download logic Self-test logic	`uctlProgressBar`	Text
`ClearProgress-` `LabelMsg`	`frmMothMain` on state changes	`uctlProgressBar`	None
`StartAuto-` `ProgressMsg`	`frmMothMain`	`ProgressBarManager` for the `uctlProgressBar`	Int secs

NewIrvPosnMsg	ucttSimRobot	uctlSimIRSensor	The Y position of the selected IR source button, minus the Top of the robot control
NewSimIRValueMsg	ucttSimIRSensor	SensorBankStub	Simulated IR value
NoSimIRMsg	ucttSimRobot	uctlSimIRSensor	None
ButtonClickedMsg	FBWButton instances	MothState instances	None
ButtonEnableMsg	MothState instances	FBWButton instances	True/false
SetCursorMsg	MothState instances	Main form	Cursor to show
CloseProgramMsg	**MothStateClosing**	Main form	None
FormClosedMsg	frmDebug	DebugButtonLink instance	Form that is closing

Table 5.5: Controls on the Main Form

Control Type	Control Name	Use
Button	btnSelfTest	Clicks initiate self-testing by all wheels
Button	btnSetup	Clicks initiate downloads of setup files to all wheels
Button	btnStartStop	Dual-use: When labeled "Start," clicks initiate tracking an IR source; when labeled "Stop," clicks stop tracking
Button	btnDebug	Clicks launch the Debug Support form

Button	btnClose	Clicks initiate closing down the program
User control uctlWheelMonitor	uctlWheelMonitorLF	Wired to display results of self-test and last speed command sent to LF wheel
User control uctlWheelMonitor	uctlWheelMonitorLR	Wired to display results of self-test and last speed command sent to LR wheel
User control uctlWheelMonitor	uctlWheelMonitorRF	Wired to display results of self-test and last speed command sent to RF wheel
User control uctlWheelMonitor	uctlWheelMonitorRR	Wired to display results of self-test and last speed command sent to RR wheel
User control uctlShowIR	uctlShowIR	Display raw IR readings and the direction of IR
User control uctlProgressBar	uctlProgressBar	Show auto-progress during self-testing; show progress during downloads

5.8 Wheel Monitor Controls

The main GUI form, `frmMothMain` (Figure 5.1), shows four instances of user control `uctlWheelMonitor`. Each instance displays information about one wheel. Each displays the results of self-testing and the last wheel-speed command sent to a wheel. Figure 5.5 illustrates the logic behind an instance of `uctlWheelMonitor`.

The form-load event handler of `frmMothMain` initializes the four instances. It wires one as a monitor for the left-front wheel, one for the left-rear, another for the right-front, and the last for the right-rear wheel. This it does by giving each `uctlWheelMonitor` the name of a wheel ("Left Front," "Left Rear," etc.) and the bus node of the wheel engine assigned to that wheel.

An instance of `uctlWheelMonitor` links handlers for two messages, `WheelSpeedMsg` sent to the given wheel engine, and `WheelSelfTestResultsMsg` sent by the given engine. Handlers for those messages simply display the payload of the message.

Figure 5.5: uctlWheelMonitor displays information about one wheel.
(Code: RobotController.uctlWheelMonitor.cs)

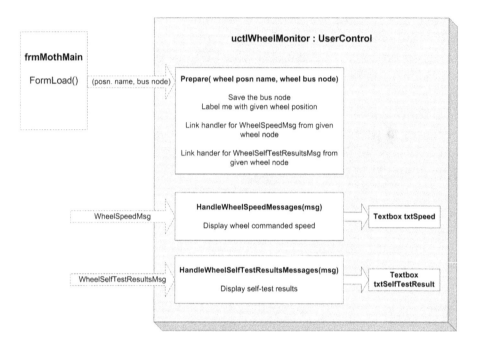

5.9 Progress Bar Control

The main GUI form, frmMothMain (Figure 5.1) shows an instance of user control uctlProgressBar, displaying progress during downloads. That control displays the progress of downloading setup files and auto progress while waiting for responses to self-test commands to the wheels. Figure 5.6 illustrates the logic behind the progress bar control.

Figure 5.6: `uctlProgressBar` on `frmMothMain` showing progress during downloading. (Code: `RobotController.uctlProgressBar.cs`)

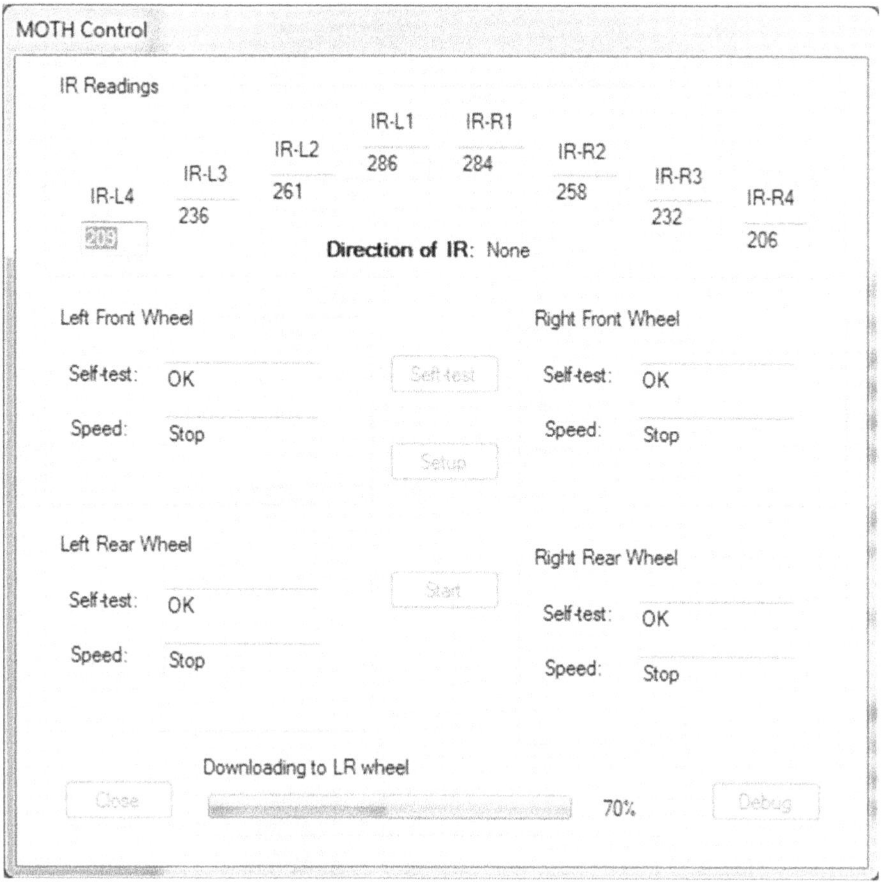

User control `uctlProgressBar` is an encapsulation of three controls: a progress bar that displays progress, a label that shows the progress as a percentage (e.g., 70 percent), and a group box whose caption answers the question, *progress of what?*

The form-load event handler of `frmMothMain` invokes the `IdentifyProgressBar()` method of the instance of `uctlProgressBar`, passing it the bus node assigned to it and text to display when no progress is under way. Internally, `uctlProgressBar` allocates an instance of `ProgressBarManager` to coordinate response to the messages that control the display of progress. It also links handlers for messages that convey text for labeling the progress, e.g., "Downloading setup information."

The instance of `ProgressBarManager` links handlers for progress-control messages: `ProgressBarClearMsg`, `ProgressBarSetMaxMsg`, `ProgressBarUpdateProgressMsg`, and `StartAutoProgressMsg`.

Progress of What?

The user control `uctlProgressBar` accepts two messages used to label the progress. The first, `LabelProgressMsg`, bears a payload that is the text to display as the caption of the `GroupBox` that encloses the progress bar, thus telling a user what the advancing progress signifies. The second message, `ClearLabelProgressMsg`, causes `uctlProgressBar` to revert to showing the default text given to the user control in its `IdentifyProgressBar` method.

Auto Progress

Self-testing uses auto-progress. The length of time that self-testing will take to complete is unknown, except that it will not exceed ten seconds. Logic that initiates wheel self-testing sends a `StartAutoProgressMsg` message to `uctlProgressBar` with a payload of ten. User control `uctlProgressBar` advances the display of progress, one-tenth of the total progress displayable, every second. When logic in the wheel engines determines that the self-tests are complete or have timed-out, `uctlProgressBar` gets a `ProgressBarClearMsg` and clears the progress.

Augmented Progress

Downloading uses augmented progress because it can quantify how much it has to do before beginning. Downloading consists of sending the lines of a text setup file to the wheel controllers. After reading in the setup file, the number of lines is known, so a `ProgressSetMaxMsg` to `uctlProgressBar` prepares the progress bar with the value that is 100 percent progress, i.e., the number of lines in the setup file. As the downloading progresses, each time a line from the file is sent, uctlProgressBar receives an instance of ProgressUpdateProgressMsg with a payload of one, so it advances the progress value by one . By the time the last line of the setup file goes to the wheel controller, the progress has been counted up to 100 percent.

Figure 5.7: uctlProgressBar displays progress for any component of the program.
(Code: RobotController.uctlProgressBar.cs)

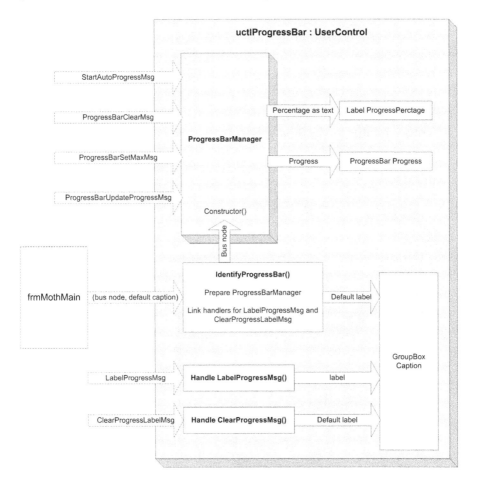

5.10 Show IR Control

The main GUI form, `frmMothMain` (Figure 5.1), shows an instance of user control `uctlShowIR`. That control displays the raw IR reading from all of the IR sensors. Figure 5.8 illustrates the logic behind the instance of `uctlShowIR`.

The `Prepare` method in `uctlShowIR` initializes the control. It links handlers for messages from the `InfraredSensors` engine. Handlers for the IR direction messages (`IRCenteredMsg`, `IRLeftPredominatesMsg`, `IRRightPredominatesMsg`, `NoIRMsg`) merely display the direction: "Centered," "Left," "Right," "None."

The other message from `InfraredSensor`, `IRReadingsMsg`, carries raw reading of IR intensity from the IR sensors. The handler in `uctlShowIR` for that message extracts the readings and displays them.

5.11 Debug Forms

WinAppInfrastructure supplies a form, `frmDebug` (Figure 5.9), to aid in debugging. That form functions as a "sniffer" on the logical bus. On the right, the form lists the names of all the logical messages defined in the program. A programmer can select any number of the message names. Each time a selected message appears on the bus, the form displays it and its payload.

Figure 5.8: uctlShowIR displays raw IR readings
(Code: RobotController.uctlShowIR.cs)

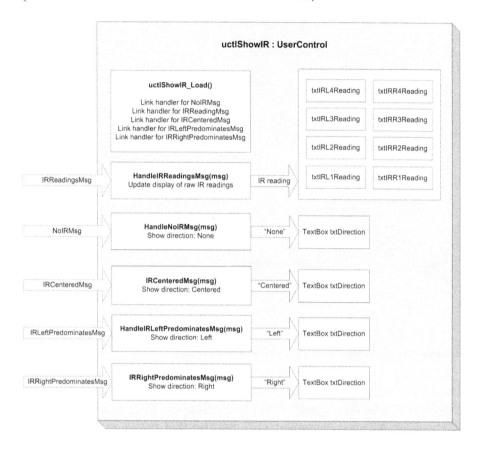

Figure 5.9: Debug Support form showing communication with wheel controllers during download of setup files. (Code: `WinAppInfrastructure.frmDebug.cs`)

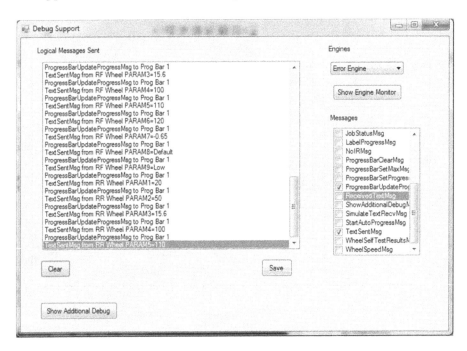

One of the logical messages is `DebugMsg`. It conveys text as its payload. That text will be displayed on the Debug Support form when `DebugMsg` is checked. As a programmer, you can use that message for whatever you like. Just include a line of code like the following wherever there is something you would like to see while the program is running:

```
new DebugMsg("No response from wheel").Send();
```

The Debug Support form also enables a programmer to see what's going on with engines and jobs. The form presents a list of all the engines defined by the program (top right). Select one, say, Left Front Wheel, and click the *Show Engine Monitor* button. The form in Figure 5.10 will appear. The form displays the status of the engine and the job it is running, if any. The one in Figure 5.10 shows that the wheel engine for the left front wheel is executing a Self-Test Wheel job.

Figure 5.10: Engine Monitor showing status of the wheel engine for the left front wheel during self-testing on that wheel (Code: `RobotController.frmEngineMonitor.cs`)

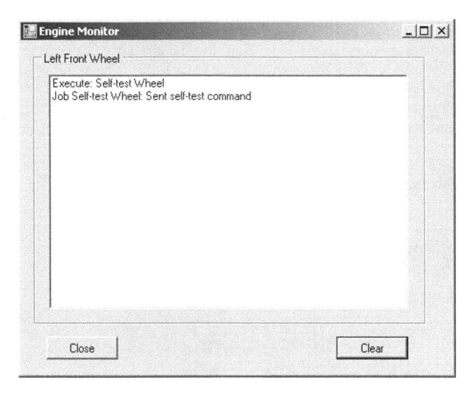

What gets displayed for the status of jobs is whatever the programmer decides. A running job can invoke a method in the engine that is running the job to update its status. The engine automatically updates its own status when it begins executing a job and when the job completes. The engine sends a message reporting the changes in status. Engine Monitor forms receive those messages and display the statuses.

Look again at the Debug Support form in Figure 5.9. Note the button *Show Additional Debug*. It provides the means to launch another debug form supplied by the application project of the solution. Click that button and the form sends a message, `ShowAdditionalDebugMsg`. FBWwinAppDemo's main form receives the message and responds by showing the *Simulate Moth* form of Figure 5.11.

The `frmSimulate` form gives us the ability to run FBWwinAppDemo and debug it even before we get the hardware. The form affects a robot in the shape of a control that moves around the form, homing in on the position of a simulated source of IR chosen by a user. As the "robot" moves, its IR sensors display readings of IR that are related to the closeness (vertically) of the sensor to the position of the selected IR source. Code in the simulated robot sends IR-direction messages (`NoIRMsg`, `IRCenteredMsg`, `IRLeftPredominatesMsg`, and `IRRightPredominatesMsg`) based on readings of IR in the eight simulated IR sensors. In response, the control program issues wheel-speed commands that turn the robot in the direction of the IR source. Coloring in the simulated sensors on the "face" of the robot indicates how "hot" they are, that is, how much IR they are picking up.

Figure 5.11: The form used to simulate the actual robot. It sends messages that simulate IR and responds, in a simulated way, to commands from the robot controller. Responding to wheel-speed commands from the controller, the simulated robot moves up, down, and forward across the form toward a (simulated) source of IR chosen by a user of the program. (Code: `RobotController.frmSimulate.cs`)

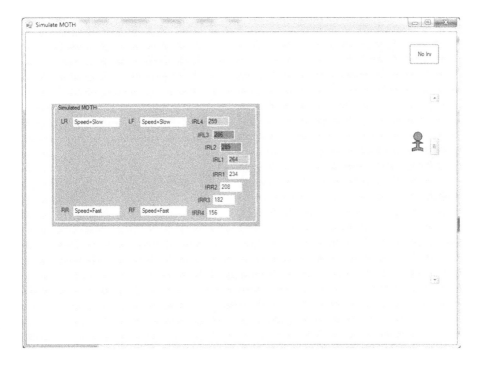

Chapter 6: Heretical Thoughts on Software Development Process

Recall the subtitle of this book: How to Write Complex but Reliable Windows Applications Quickly. *Quickly* . My claim is that the fly-by-wire architecture will help you to do this. But all the productivity resulting from this choice of architecture, and from the skill and creativity of the programmers who implement it, can be squandered–ground into dust and washed down the sewer—by the typical process for software development.

After thirty-five years in the software development business, I have some opinions about how best to conduct it. I include them here for your consideration. You may enjoy learning that you are not crazy, that there are better ways to do this job—ways that accord with your instincts and creative sensibilities.

6.1 Discovering Your Design

Software development is an iterative process. The final design of a program is in a strange way more of a discovery than a creation. If you want good software, you will not be afraid to start over two, three, or four times. This is necessary because as you elaborate your ideas, you find that they lead to contortions, awkwardness, and hacks. When this happens, you must back up and come at it again.

Very little of my work from the first months of a year-long programming effort is in the finished product. It gets factored out. It is overtaken by deeper insights and morphed into derivations of a smaller, simpler set of assumptions.

What comes to pass is similar to what happens to scientific theories, as explained by philosopher of science Thomas Kuhn in his 1962 classic, *The Structure of Scientific Revolutions*. In this book, Kuhn coined the term "paradigm shift" to describe what must periodically take place in scientific theory as experiments designed to test hypotheses become increasingly precise.

If a hypothesis is good, the first (crude) experiments designed to test it, confirm it. That is, the experiments find what the theory predicts will be found, to a degree of precision afforded by the sensitivity of measurement employed in the experiment. Subsequent rounds of more precise testing may also confirm the hypothesis to a few more decimal places.

In time, however, investigators make observations that do not accord with what the hypothesis predicts. If the discrepancies are not too great, some tweaks may make the predictions align with what is observed. Eventually, though, no amount of tweaking will make the predictions match observations, or so much tweaking will produce an unsatisfying—ugly—theory. In either case, it is back to the drawing board.

Back at the drawing board, theorists start over. They take a completely different approach, adopt a new paradigm. The Ptolemaic solar system (earth-centered), for instance, gives way to the Copernican solar system (sun-centered). Even incorrectly assuming circular orbits (instead of the actual elliptical orbits), the Copernican model yields more accurate calculations of the paths of the planets. The shift from Newtonian gravity as motive force to Einstein's curved space-time improves the predictions even more.

Einstein's theory is, of course, radically more abstract. Its advantage is that its assumptions lead to correct predictions. For example, while Newtonian calculations yield a prediction for the rate of precession of the perihelion of Mercury's orbit (Figure 6.1) that differs from observations by some forty-three arc-seconds per century, Einstein's slide rule gives a number that matches observation, within the margin of error of the measurement.

Figure 6.1: The precession of Mercury's orbit. The orbit shifts in its plane a little bit every year, and in 2250 centuries its perihelion (the point at which the planet passes nearest the sun) makes a complete rotation around the sun. The diagram illustrates the shift in orbital path over about 280 centuries. The influence of the other planets in the solar system causes the precession, but calculations of their effect assuming Newton's tug of gravity yield the wrong value for the rate of rotation. Recalculations after the paradigm shift to Einstein's conception of warped space-time give the correct answer.

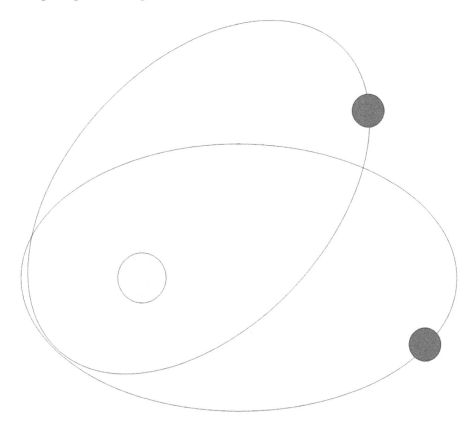

Software development is like this—an iterative process. It is exploration of ideas to discover their implications, a process of sifting, refining, simplifying, distilling. Counter-intuitively, it takes longer to write a program of ten thousand lines of code than to achieve the same result with twenty thousand lines. As dear Pascal said in apologizing for the length of a letter: "I didn't have time to make it shorter." The class, or method, that will never have a bug and does not need to be tested, is the one you design *out* of the program.

If this depiction of software development is surprising, now comes a shocking observation: the elaboration of your thoughts for the design of a program is most quickly done in code. It is through coding, not detailed design, that you rapidly explore the implications of your ideas, traverse a series of paradigms, and uncover an elegant design. This is because code is the only rendering of your ideas precise enough to show you the dead-ends. Consequently, the most helpful tool in the quest to find your design is a compiler.

This is heresy, I know. The modern formal development process calls for a phase of detailed design, after settling on the overall architecture, before coding begins. Detailed design lays out the program in increasing detail, generally using graphical tools. The problem is that many ideas must be pushed all the way to the bottom to see where they lead. Detailed design methods, such as Unified Modeling Language (UML) are just too cumbersome and unwieldy to do this rapidly.

There is another way in which software development practice differs from theory. In theory you get to begin with detailed requirements for your program, written by the stakeholders in its success. Stakeholders are people in your organization—people from marketing, manufacturing, quality control, service—who have opinions about how the program should end up working and looking.

Unfortunately, those people are busy. They are too busy to generate testable requirements for your software. You can probably bring them together in a conference room with a blackboard for an hour-long kick off meeting, but they will be too busy to give more than superficial attention to your requests for feedback on your initial ideas.

This means your first effort will be a prototype. In general you cannot get the stakeholder's attention until you have something to show them, something about which you can say: this is it; speak now or forever hold your peace. At that point, they will speak. With something to look at, something to focus on, something to demonstrate, you'll be able to keep their attention and gain their criticism.

This is not as bad as it sounds because it allows you to write the program twice. You must regard the prototype as a *learning experience*, and you must *set it aside and start over*. The second iteration will go much, much faster because the first attempt allowed you to see all the way to the bottom, and you begin the second effort armed with actual input from the stakeholders. In fact, *the knowledge gained from doing the prototype permits you to rapidly complete a detailed design before commencing the rewrite of the program*, if such is your preference.

This may seem as if it will double the cost of producing the program. It won't. *Write-it-twice is the fastest way to get a reliable program*. But this is true only if you think of the first product as a learning experience and lay it aside. Otherwise, you'll be hacking on your initial prototype until management shoots the engineers and ships a buggy product, a year late.

6.2 Coding Standards

Most software development organizations have what are called *coding standards*. Coding standards describe good programming practice and contain a great many rules for how code should look. The idea is to get code of a single style and appearance from all the programmers on a project.

This sounds reasonable, but programmers famously resist adhering to coding standards. Project managers rarely ask, why? Well, did Michelangelo conform to painting standards supplied by his patrons? (Actually, I don't know, but I hope not.) Did Picasso or Warhol? Am I suggesting that programming is as much art as science, subject to aesthetic considerations? Yes, I am.

Experienced programmers don't wish to program willy-nilly. If left to themselves, they follow standards—their own. They tend to feel that an organization's coding standards are generally just the prejudices of the programmers who worked there before they did.

More practically, consistently formatted code contains clues that make it immediately intelligible to its author while he scans it. Every experienced programmer has his own way of achieving this result through formatting style. Unfortunately, the clues in somebody else's style may go unrecognized, requiring more of a deliberate and time-consuming effort to navigate through that code.

So every programmer's short answer is: coding standards are great, as long as they're mine. I agree. See the Appendix for mine.

6.3 Testing

Developer testing

Software developers test their code as they complete pieces of it. To do this they run the program that includes the code and observe its behavior. This is called developer-testing. It is not systematic, that is, not driven by written test procedures that attempt to verify the operation of the piece of code against written requirements for it. Its purpose is merely to weed out the obvious bugs before commencing systematic testing.

Developer-testing may not be systematic, but it can be thorough. Experienced programmers spend significant time satisfying themselves that a piece of code functions as they envision. They cause the program to run in ways that exercise the code in every manner it can come into play. They arrange for the code to see good data, bad data, maybe no data, and see that it does the correct thing in every case.

The details of how this is done are up to the developer. Often you temporarily hack another part of the program to feed your code good data, change the hack to give bad data, and change it again to send no data. Finally, you remove the hacks. Because the hacks come out once you're satisfied, you have to repeat these steps to repeat the testing. But the advantage is that you can do all of this fairly quickly.

Systematic testing

What is not quick is systematic testing. Systematic testing proceeds according to a written plan. The plan dictates actions designed to verify that the software meets every one of its written requirements.

To get an insight into systematic testing, let's borrow a term from the military, namely, "set-piece." Two opposing armies sometimes move themselves into position for face-to-face combat. They deploy their artillery, armor, and infantry and pound each other in place. This is known as a set-piece battle—"set-piece" because it is not a battle of maneuver but a fight between prepared positions of situated weapons, principally artillery whose individual guns are called pieces. Think of WWI in Europe. Set-piece battles are often months in the planning, preparation, and execution.

Let us now speak of set-piece testing. I refer to testing efforts mounted with significant planning and preparation. They often involve the creation of software "fixtures" or "harnesses," if you will. These are additions to the program, or additional programs that provide the means to stimulate the software under test and monitor and possibly record its behavior. With all this in place, a person runs through a written test procedure that serves to excite the program in every possible way. The person may record the outcome of each step of the test, or the software fixtures may.

In a sense, the hacks that programmers use in developer-testing are software fixtures, but they are quickly conceived and used and disappear once a programmer is satisfied with what they reveal about the code he is testing. This is not true of the fixtures and procedures employed in set-piece testing. So much work goes into the preparation of set-piece testing that it must be repeatable. You can to it today and find bugs and do it again after the bugs have been fixed without having to recreate the plans, procedures, or fixtures.

Something that adds to the time it takes to prepare for set-piece testing is the fact that the procedures and fixtures themselves must be tested. The more powerful and complicated the procedures and software you create to help test other software, the more you have to consider the possibility that apparent anomalies arise from problems with the procedures or side effects of the testing software, rather than from the tested software. You will expend considerable time in checking and debugging the assets employed in set-piece testing.

Systematic testing is what I have been calling set-piece testing. It can be of great value, but is quite costly. Consequently, I recommend that it be used where it is most effective.

End-to-end testing

Systematic testing is clearly indicated for end-to-end testing. In this kind of testing, you think of the program in its entirety as a "black box" whose behavior as an entity is specified. For a given stimulus, or set of stimuli, there is a correct response from the program.

End-to-end testing brings with it one great simplification. Software fixtures for it, if any, are nonintrusive. You may write and use programs in the testing, but they are outside; you never include anything in the software under test. You don't because it is all about how the software functions as a whole. We're really not so concerned about supposed bugs in the code if they never manifest themselves in anomalous behavior by the program. You still have to worry about the programs you create to stimulate and monitor the program under test, but gone is the possibility that testing code within the program will affect it.

There is another reason why the systematic approach works well for end-to-end testing. Systematic testing necessitates that requirements exist for the thing being tested, and if there are going to be requirements for anything, it will be for the functioning of the program as a whole.

Unit testing

Modern software development process calls upon us to use the systematic approach for unit testing as well. Think of your program as resulting from the integration of all of its components, or units. Unit testing refers to checking each of the components in isolation.

In unit testing, you extract a single module for evaluation. You embed that module in an artificial environment that recreates everything about the actual program that the module depends on or affects, making the artificial environment something you can manipulate during testing. Testing consists of manipulating the environment in all the ways necessary to exercise everything about the single module under test.

If this sounds like a lot of work, it is. This is set-piece testing of the most demanding kind.

Whether unit testing repays the effort depends on whether you go overboard in identifying the units needing systematic evaluation. It is reasonable to designate as units needing testing all the boxes representing software on the diagram of the program's architecture. But it is not uncommon for a program to have one thousand classes or more, and if you regard each class as a unit requiring a set-piece testing effort, you can forget about completing the project on-time and under-budget.

The fly-by-wire architecture makes unit testing more feasible. In a program structured like this, you test modules by sending them messages from unit-test code. A tester interacts with the unit-test code to drive the testing. The module-under-test doesn't know that the messages coming to it are part of a testing effort, so it responds as it is programmed to, and a tester observes its response.

Integration testing

Integration testing refers to checking the interaction among the units of the program. Checking occurs during developer testing, of course, but modern software-development process asks us to perform systematic integration testing, too.

Here again, whether this is smart depends on whether you follow my advice about unit testing. If you limit your idea of units to the high-level components of your program, then systematic testing of their interactions is a reasonable thing to do, especially because there is some likelihood that somebody wrote detailed requirements for the high-level components of the program.

In summary, my recommendations concerning testing are as follows:

1) Recognize that systematic testing, done right, is time consuming and expensive and can't proceed without written requirements for the things to be tested.

2) Insist on thorough developer testing.

3) Consider systematic unit testing of the highest-level components.

4) Consider systematic integration testing for the highest-level components.

5) Reserve a large part of the project budget for systematic end-to-end testing; no amount of unit and integration testing can substitute for thorough end-to-end testing.

6.4 Define "Done"

I once met a man who worked in a brass foundry. Castings came to him after they had cooled and undergone some light machining. His job was to polish them. He showed me the shiny pieces still in his care, and I asked, "How do you know when you're done?" "Done?" he asked in reply. "I'm never done; I just keep polishing until they take them away."

Sound familiar? When do you call a program "done"?

The first answer is that a program is done when it can't be improved. That's a pretty high standard. Unfortunately, the only other answer is, when it's good enough. No one likes to think of his work as "good enough," but "can't be improved" is something you approach only asymptotically. As they say in the parts-procurement business, perfection has a long lead time.

Actually, with reference to Section 6.1, the further you push it, the more likely you are to run into an intractable imperfection which you can address only with another paradigm shift. Of course, the write-it-twice methodology reduces the chance of this happening late in the effort: you use what you learn from a first rendering of the program to inform a quicker, better rewrite that begins with full knowledge of the destination.

Still, most programmers become emotionally invested in their code. I know I do. Managers generally have to pry a project from our cold, dead fingers. I can generally let go after a two- or three-week vacation. When I return, I have equanimity enough to fashion the needed compromises and call it done.

But I have seen a more formal way of accomplishing this. Some shops employ teams of starters and finishers. The starters begin the project and bring it a point beyond "basically working," perhaps to the mythical "90 percent complete" milestone. When their productivity plateaus, when they, like Flaubert, are spending the morning putting in a comma and the afternoon taking it out, they get a new project to begin, and the finishers come in to wrap things up. The finishers join the project with no baggage. They are judged on their ability to get the software out the door, bug free—so that is what they do.

Closely related to the question of what does "done" mean is another question: how long will it take? The first point about estimating effort is that you get out of it what you put into it. You can spend an hour, a day, or a week generating an estimate. You'll get what you pay for.

Moreover, I have found that experienced programmers can estimate fairly accurately how long it will take to get to a program that is basically working. Unfortunately, that will be at most two-thirds of the total effort.

6.5 Killing Trees

Modern software development process generates a lot of paper. It is not uncommon to wind up with one page of documentation for every five lines of code. For a ten thousand-line program, that's (I'll do the math) two thousand pages of documentation.

All work proceeds according to written plans. The team working on the project reviews all work products—all documents and modules of code. The findings of the reviews are recorded, and the actions undertaken in response to the findings are also recorded. They are then checked, and the findings of the checking are recorded.

So the paper output of the project includes (take a deep breath): project plans, progress reports, requirements and design documents, numerous reports of reviews of requirements and design documents and code, testing plans, test procedures, review reports for testing plans and test procedures, and numerous rounds of test reports. If you follow the rule of thumb that 80 percent of your code-creation effort goes into detailed design and 20 percent into actual coding, the detailed design must be very detailed indeed and will account for perhaps half of the two thousand pages.

But it can't hurt, right? Well, there will be an average number of errors per page. That average will be higher the more pages there are because people's eyes glaze over at some point, and they can take in only so much. The average errors per page also goes up over time because changes will happen elsewhere, and no one will remember to reflect those changes in the two thousand pages of documentation.

But despite the minor errors, the documentation is better because of the process, right? Well, consider military technical manuals (TMs). Every piece of equipment fielded by the military—weapons, radios, vehicles, mobile labs, you name it—comes with a large set of TMs written by the manufacturers of the equipment. Defense contractors employ a very rigorous process in the creation of TMs. They are still crap.

The incidence of actual errors in TMs is probably low. Nevertheless, they are often badly formatted, disjointed, lacking in context, and vague. It is clear that individual TMs derive from templates because many sections contain perfunctory verbiage that is obviously there only in order to have some black ink in all the white spaces.

But despite the lack of perfection in these documents, the process makes them better, right? Maybe, but it is a mistake to imagine that process can substitute for judgment and experience, for talent, by attempting to make the process itself a state-machine.

6.6 The Dark Side of Process

Ironically, the burden of process can be so great that it leads management to decide to ship products with defects that are technically easy to fix. The best example of this effect is a piece of industrial control equipment produced by a major manufacturer some years ago. The device had a keyboard and displayed what you typed. The odd thing about it was that when you wanted the device to accept what you had just finished typing, you hit the ESC key. When you wanted to discard your input, you hit the ENTER key.

I'm sure you can imagine how frustrating it was to use that product. It also made one wonder what else might be wrong with it. Sadly, though, I'll bet a programmer could have fixed this problem in half an hour, including time to drink and recycle a can of Mountain Dew. Nevertheless, the company decided that the cost of turning its process crank on the fix was too great and resigned itself to live with the defect.

Am I saying that process has no value? Of course not. But to begin to understand the limits of that value, consider some conversation overheard during a meeting to review a document:

"I, ah, didn't have to time to look at it closely, so..."

"Couldn't we rewrite this whole section to get rid of the passive voice..."

"I think you know what we mean here, but it is hard to, ah, it's complicated; you can work out the details..."

"I'm not sure these figures add any information, maybe..."

"But the template document calls for figures like these..."

"Whatever..."

"I see you have filled in this V&V protocol document electronically. That won't do. You have to print out the document just as I gave it to you, then use a blue or black pen to write in your observations and circle 'pass' or 'fail' at each step"... "But I have too many observations to record them by hand"... "Then write smaller or make fewer observations."

"It's eleven o'clock; I have another meeting. Does anybody see any problems with the second half of the document? No? Good. I think we are done here."

One programmer at the meeting doesn't say much. Bill's mind is on his own work, which he had to put down in order to prepare for and participate in this meeting. His foot taps under the conference-room table as he struggles to suppress thoughts of his own code. He is like Ernest Hemingway who fought to turn off his mind when the words were coming to him while he was not near his typewriter, because once they formed in his head, some part of his mind would be satisfied and be unable to conjure them again.

Bill does his duty, but he can't get excited about reviewing others' work. Reviewing has little creative component. It does not engage Bill's artistic sensibilities. He yearns to return to his canvas and the kind of fulfilling work that engineering is meant to be.

Appendix: Coding Standards

We've all had the experience of looking at code and saying, "Holy crap! I'll never understand this." As much as anything, I'm advocating a style of programming that minimizes this reaction by producing code that feels less daunting. That feeling comes from a sense that the coder took care with the work, making its appearance restful on the eyes through simplicity and regularity.

Left-margin discipline

The most helpful thing you can do to make your code less intimidating is to avoid a ragged left margin. Figure A1 shows code with a ragged left margin. Contrast it with the code in Figures A2 and A4 for a sense of what I mean by restful on the eye. Indentation from the left margin connotes logical dependency. So a very ragged left margin screams complexity.

There are several techniques for keeping the left margin regular. Begin by using indentation only to signify logical dependency upon the line above. Then, minimize the use of if-statements. Fashion each method to do a particular thing, not sometimes this thing and other times that thing based on flags. The effect of the execution of the method will differ based on inputs (arguments or properties set from outside), but, ideally, the logic of the method should not branch based on inputs.

Object-oriented programming is very helpful with this. When you need a class to function in one way when allocated for use by some code and another way when allocated for use by other code, derive two versions of it from a base class. Have the two versions override a virtual or abstract method with different logic, and employ one version in one place and the other version in another.

At the very least, don't do this:

```
bool bFoo = false;
if (<expression that evaluates to true or false>)
```

```
{
    bFoo = true;
}
else
{
    bFoo = false;
}
```

Do this instead:

```
bool bFoo = (<expression that evaluates to true or false);
```

Hide the details

When you are implementing code to achieve an inherently complex result, there will be complexity, but you have to spread it out.

One way to do this is to collect low-level details in a new class and snap an instance of that class into your higher level logic. In Figure A2, a lot of detail from A1 has been moved into another class—MyConvert . This permits people to follow your main logic without getting bogged down in details. When they need to know the details, they can go there. This technique also gives you the ability to employ the logic in the new class elsewhere in the program without reproducing it.

There is another way to hide excessive detail. Whenever an algorithm operates only on the properties of a given object, make that algorithm a method of the class of that object, give the method a name that suggests what it does, and have it return the result of executing the logic.

Hard-coding

Hard-coding refers to embedding numeric or string literals in your code, as opposed to defining names for them and using the definitions. Every coding standard ever written condemns the practice in the strongest possible terms. But honoring the admonition strictly becomes absurd. I have seen code that defines a constant,

NUMBER_TO_DIVIDE_BY_WHEN_AVERAGING_TWO_ NUMBERS = 2,

so as to avoid having the number 2 appear in the code where an average of two numbers is taken.

The only real problem is hard-coding in two or more places a fact that might change. If a piece of code employs a magic number—a scaling factor, say—and code elsewhere needs to undo the scaling for whatever reason, you don't want the magic number repeated, because if you need to change it, you might not remember that it is specified in two places.

As another example, suppose code in one place passes to other code commands that are indicated by the strings "Start" and "Stop." If the receiving code does string comparisons to "Start" and "Stop" to decide which command it got, that logic will fail if the sending code is updated to use the strings "Begin" and "End," unless the receiving code is similarly modified. Better to define START_CMD = "Start" and STOP_ CMD = "Stop" and use those definitions in both places.

But when the magic number or string appears in one place only, it is not clearly better to assign it a name and use the name in its place. Sometimes I would like to see this:

```
DisplayErrorMsg("No response from wheel controller");
```

rather than

```
class ErrorMsgs
{
    public const string ERR_MSG_NO_RSPNS_FROM_WHEEL_CNTRLR =
    "No response from wheel controller";
}

class WheelController
{
    ...
    DisplayErrorMsg(ErrorMsgs.ERR_MSG_NO_RSPNS_FROM_WHEEL_CNTRLR);
}
```

Again, this kind of hard-coding is acceptable when the value is used in one place only.

One exit

More than one exit from a method is another practice that is held in low regard by nearly all compendiums of coding standards. People believe that the one-exit rule makes code more intelligible. But what about when it doesn't? I use multiple exits from methods, but not out of sloppiness. I do it when, in my judgment, it makes the code clearer.

It is, of course, confusing to exit a method from a place in the logic more than two tabs from the left margin or from within a loop. But I contend that disposing of certain cases by exiting early from a method makes the code easier to grasp, not harder, because it permits the code that follows to stay closer to the left margin—that is, subject to less logical dependency.

Comments

Comments are essential for understanding any code.

Begin each module with a comment block that describes the purpose of the module:

```
//**********************************************************
// Represent a wheel controller
//**********************************************************
```

Introduce each method with a comment block. In unconditional and FBW programming, it is often not necessary to know how execution gets to a piece of code (you can wring it out when you feel you must), but only what it does when it runs. So the most important information in an introductory comment block for a method is context, supplied by a statement of why or when the method executes and descriptions of its arguments. Explain what the method *does* using comments in the body of the method. The introductory comments should also describe what the method returns, if anything.

For example:

```
//*******************************************************
///<summary>Runs when a debilitating error occurs</summary>
///<param name="objErr">Information about the error</param>
//*******************************************************
private void OnDebilitatingError(object objErr)
{
    // signal the remainder of the program to shutdown
    WinAppProgramControl.Shutdown();

    // show the a description of the error
    ((WinAppError)objErr).Show();

    // end the program by closing this, the main form
    this.Close();
}
```

Remember that comments are not checked by a compiler, so they often become out of date if code they describe is changed. So don't use comments to state things about the code that a reviewer can easily see for himself; don't restate exactly what the code does, but rather the intention or effect of executing the code:

```
// enable sending if the user has entered characters that
// represent a valid integer
this.btnSend.Enabled = MyConvert.IsInteger(this.txtSN.Text);
```

Use blank lines to separate code into groups of lines that work together to achieve an intermediate result within the method. Introduce each grouping with a comment describing what the lines together accomplish.

Scope

Scope refers to the visibility of a program element to other parts of the program. Make scope as restrictive as possible. If a class, method, property, or event is not needed outside the module that contains it, make it *private*. If it is not needed outside of the project that contains the module, make it *internal*.

The *internal* scope is most useful when making a class library. Usually, the most esoteric methods and properties of a class can remain private, but sometimes access to them is needed from outside. To limit the potential for misuse of these features, make their scope *internal* whenever possible. This makes them available to programmers working inside the library, programmers who are more likely to be familiar with its more abstruse workings, but not to users of the library, who would be more likely to misunderstand and misuse them.

Length of control structures

You want to keep the bodies of control structures (if-then-else and loops) short enough that you can see the opening brace and closing brace on the screen at the same time. Ideally the IF and the ELSE causes are fully visible together on one screen.

Wired

I want my code to convey a sense of being "wired." People should see it as reactive, not contemplative. No one should imagine the code as thinking or deciding. The thinking went into the design of the wiring, and the wiring just reacts.

Again, figure A2 furnishes a good example. The Send button's Enable property is wired to the text-box control's text field by this simple code. The wiring is achieved, without branching, by means of another class (which may include branching) that is snapped into the main logic.

That example also illustrates another technique that suggests wiring. Note that the Send button remains disabled until the information that would be sent is valid. So there is no possibility of the user asking to send information that is not valid and, therefore, no need to check the information when the send-click comes and no need for an error message if the information is invalid when the click comes.

Figure A3 also presents code written to appear "wired." The constructor of a module that represents a right wheel of the robot links handlers for messages that report the direction of IR, and the handlers reflexively command the wheel to run at speeds that make the robot turn toward the IR source.

Figure A1: Illustrate code with a ragged left margin.

```
//*******************************************************
///<summary>Runs when the user types in the Serial Number
///text box</summary>
//*******************************************************
private void SerialNumber_TextChanged1(object sender, EventArgs e)
{
    bool bIsInt = false;

    // see if user has entered a valid integer as the serial number
    string strText = this.txtSerialNumber.Text;

    if (strText != "")
    {
        try
        {
            Convert.ToInt32(strText);
            bIsInt = true;
        }
        catch
        {
            bIsInt = false;
        }
    }
    // enable sending if the user has entered characters that
    // represent a valid integer
    this.btnSend.Enabled = bIsInt;
}
```

Figure A2: Illustrate the same functionality as Figure A1, but with a wired and restful look.

```
//*******************************************************
///<summary>Runs when the user types in the Serial Number text
///box</summary>
//*******************************************************
private void SN_TextChanged(object sender, EventArgs e)
{
    // enable sending if the user has entered characters that
    //represent a valid integer

    this.btnSend.Enabled = MyConvert.IsInteger(this.txtSN.Text);
}
```

Figure A3: Wired-looking code. The constructor links handlers for logical messages that reflexively command wheel speeds that make the robot turn toward the IR source.

```
//*********************************************************
//*********************************************************
///<summary>Represents a left wheel</summary>
//*********************************************************
//*********************************************************
internal class LeftWheel : Wheel
{
    //*****************************************************
    ///<summary>Constructs a certain left wheel</summary>
    ///<param name="enmMyNode">Bus node of the wheel</param>
    ///<param name="strComPort">COM port connected to the wheel
    // controller</param>
    ///<param name="strName">Name of the wheel</param>
    //*****************************************************
    public LeftWheel(string name, BusNode myNode, string comPort)
        : base(strName, enmMyNode, strComPort)
    {
        // left wheels will go at slow speed when IR dominates on left
        LogicalBus.RegisterMessageHandler
        (typeof(IRLeftPredominatesMsg), this.DoSlowRotation);

        // left wheels will go at normal speed when IR dominates
        // on right
        LogicalBus.RegisterMessageHandler(
            typeof(IRRightPredominatesMsg), this.DoNormalRotation);
    }

    //*****************************************************
    ///<summary>Handles a message about direction of IR that should
    ///cause wheel to run slow</summary>
    //*****************************************************
    protected void DoSlowRotation(LogicalMessage objMsg)
    { this.SendWheelSpeed("Slow"); }

    //*****************************************************
    ///<summary>Handles a msg about direction of IR that should cause
    ///this wheel to normal</summary>
    ///<param name="objMsg">Not used</param>
    //*****************************************************
    protected void DoNormalRotation(LogicalMessage objMsg)
    { this.SendWheelSpeed("Fast"); }
```

}

Figure A4: Restful and "wired-looking" code. Not only is the left margin straight, the right end of lines exhibit a restful pattern.

```
private Signal mobjNoIREvent = new Signal();
private Signal mobjIRLeftEvent = new Signal();
private Signal mobjIRRightEvent = new Signal();
private Signal mobjIRCenteredEvent = new Signal();

// minimum IR value that is meaningful
private const int MIN_READING = 10;

// minimum meaningful difference in IR intensity between left and right
private const int TOLERANCE = 10;

//**************************************************************
///<summary>Constructs and instance</summary>
//**************************************************************
public IRSensors()
{
    // link handlers for signals that announce the direction of IR
    this.mobjIRCenteredEvent.LinkHandler(this.OnIRCenteredEvent);
    this.mobjIRRightEvent.LinkHandler(this.OnIRRightEvent);
    this.mobjIRLeftEvent.LinkHandler(this.OnIRLeftEvent);
    this.mobjNoIREvent.LinkHandler(this.OnNoIREvent);
}


//**************************************************************
///<summary>Read the IR sensors and cause messages to be sent that
///indicate the direction of the IR source and the values read from
///each sensor</summary>
//**************************************************************
public void ReadSensors()
{
    // read the channels
    base.LatchReadings();

    // sum the left and right readings
    int intLeftSum = this.SumSensors(0, 4);
    int intRghtSum = this.SumSensors(4, 4);

    // flag no IR seen
    bool bNoIR = ((intLeftSum == 0) && (intRghtSum == 0));

    // flag that there is more IR on the left
    bool bLeft = (intLeftSum > (intRghtSum + TOLERANCE));

    // flag that there is more IR on the right
    bool bRght = (intRghtSum > (intLeftSum + TOLERANCE));
```

```
    // flag that IR is centered
    bool bCentered = (!bLeft && !bRght && !bNoIR);

    // announce where the IR source is
    this.mobjNoIREvent.FireIfTrue(bNoIR);
    this.mobjIRLeftEvent.FireIfTrue(bLeft);
    this.mobjIRRightEvent.FireIfTrue(bRght);
    this.mobjIRCenteredEvent.FireIfTrue(bCentered);
}

//****************************************************************
// Send messages to announce where the IR source is
//****************************************************************
private void OnNoIREvent(object objArg)
{ new NoIRMsg().Send(); }

private void OnIRCenteredEvent(object objArg)
{ new IRCenteredMsg().Send(); }

private void OnIRLeftEvent(object objArg)
{ new IRLeftPredominatesMsg().Send(); }

private void OnIRRightEvent(object objArg)
{ new IRRightPredominatesMsg().Send();} }
```